The Secret Life of People

Jo Robinson

ISBN eBook 978 0-6399488-7-4 non-fiction

ISBN Paperback 978-0-6399488-8-1 non-fiction

Weaverback Press

Published by Weaverback Press
89 Anderson St - Unit 6, Louis Trichardt, 0920, South Africa
+27 15 516 8158 +27 63 319 1421

This book is designed to provide information, entertainment, and motivation, and contains the sole opinions of the author. It is not meant to be used, nor should it be used, to diagnose or treat any medical condition. For diagnosis or treatment for any medical or mental health condition, please consult a physician. It is sold with the understanding that the publisher and author are not engaged to render any type of psychological, legal, or any other kind of professional advice. No warrantees or guarantees are expressed or implied by any of this book's content. Neither the publisher nor the author shall be liable for any physical, psychological, emotional, financial, or commercial damages, including, but not limited to, special, incidental, consequential or other damages.

Dedication

This book is dedicated to people who I will not name, but who inspired me to finish it. I almost did not, weighed down by thoughts of *Who do you think you are to be sharing all of these things that you found?* Even after years of meeting so many people who had lived lives somewhere on a scale from quiet desperation to outright heart-shattering breakdown, who did not seem to have any idea of how to begin to fix themselves because they did not understand what was ailing them, I was still reluctant to share any of my personal revelations. Until I met the one who made me cry so hard I realized that the question should have been *Who are you **not** to share all of these things that you have found?* My gratitude goes out to those of you who made me understand that when you are helped, you must pay it forward. This is not the time in the history of this world and of humanity to withhold anything that could make even the smallest contribution in slowing the dangerous downward spiral on the path to destruction that we are now on.

There is a war going on, and you are the prize.

Preface

Three questions that most humans would love to have definite answers to are, who am I, what am I, and why am I? Some of the possible answers to those questions are terrifying, and so are generally not thought about much or in great detail. They are often avoided to the point of harm to self or others. People "live" internally, and do not realise how very much alike we all are in our quests not to be seen as weird, bad, or crazy. It usually comes as a surprise when another admits to the same quirks and sins we take so much care to hide about ourselves. Even so, we are now in a time where more and more of us are sharing our genuine desire to help save our world and each other in any small way that we can, even if that means exposing our own most personal experiences.

As people begin to go within and discover truths about themselves, they are also becoming very much more aware of the terrible state we humans have got ourselves into, and the equally terrible state that we have got the whole world into in the process. We realise that the time for change is now. Right now. But even if the best way to begin to change the world is to change ourselves, it can appear too overwhelming and pointless to try in the face of and on the scale of the surrounding chaos. We must learn that our one small change will be part of a great many changes taking place. A vital part. And hope that it is still possible to save ourselves and the world around us before we hit the point of no return, even though that point is alarmingly close. This is why the time has come for us to make every effort to find out who and what we are, and why it is so important that we make full use of the lives we have before it is too late.

Many are waking up to the fact that there should be a better way to live. A fact that has become so glaringly obvious it is amazing that some people still insist that the way that they are living is just fine regardless of any consequences, and they will certainly not change without a fight. For the rest of us, once aware of this fact, it becomes almost impossible to prevent trying to find a way to *do life* just a little bit differently. Truth is the key. When you see the world as it is, without sugar-coating anything, the good and the bad, and when you see yourself as you really are, you realise that it is not only possible to have a better life, but that it is essential to strive to do so. Knowledge is power. It really is. Life on Earth is not an easy journey for most, but it can be much easier when undertaken with purpose. With the strength that comes from embracing your individuality, and the conscious choice to make this life a meaningful trip. First you have to understand. First you must look, and when looking becomes hard, you must remember that you are much more powerful than you may think you are, and then keep looking until you know as much as you can. The end result is worth it.

The majority of people in the world are now living in constant stress, believing that this is normal and acceptable because everyone else is doing it. Stress related problems such as physical immune disorders and mental and spiritual illnesses, including depression, anxiety and personality disorders which sometimes lead to suicide or breakdown, are on the rise. Around four percent of the population are believed to be sociopaths (one in twenty-five people), most of them walking among us without our knowledge of what they are, and this number also is on the rise. Suddenly a great many people are noticing that things are not as they should be. This is because we truly cannot lie to ourselves at our core. We can cover the truth for a time, but not forever. Our world has become a traumatic place for every being on it.

Stockholm Syndrome is a fascinating mental aberration. When a person is held hostage, generally in a traumatic situation that they cannot (or believe they cannot) get out of, in order to try and protect themselves, they develop a (false but real to them) respect or affection for whoever it is that has them stuck in that horrible situation. They develop an alliance with their jailers, and even feel sympathy for them. This way people pretend that evil is good and acceptable because actually recognising and accepting the evil that is being done is too painful to bear when they believe that there is no chance of escape. People do this not only in situations of physical captivity, but also in cases of mental and spiritual abuse situations that they cannot change or run away from. Victims will often defend their captors, and can behave rather aggressively towards anyone who they perceive as wanting to harm their abusers with words or deeds.

Strange as this may sound, humanity as a whole seems to be suffering from a collective form of Stockholm Syndrome. We are born into a world with few visible choices. We must conform to the society that we find ourselves in. We must work and have homes to live in. We must obey rules that we had no part in creating and do not necessarily agree with. We are brought up to believe what we are taught, and to behave the way that our parents, caregivers, and teachers want us to behave. We are born into a prison that masquerades as freedom. But to say that or take action to stop it from happening could get us into a lot of trouble. So we must find a way to accept it, live with it, and *like* it. We pay it forward to our own children. We feel obligated to trust our rulers, because not to would mean accepting that we are not free, and that somewhere along the way we have made some very large mistakes in choosing or allowing our current society to exist. We truly believe that we *need* our rulers. Apart from the outright despots and dictators around the world, we generally admire, or at least respect our rulers whether we like them or not. This is regardless of the fact that most of them are much more concerned with their own financial and other goals than the betterment of any populace. We believe that humans are not good enough to ever live without strict rules and controls in place. We are terrified of anarchy, and we believe that we must keep the "safety" of our world just the way it is.

We do our best to avoid what we *know* in that place within all of us that cannot lie. We try never to see that our rulers are mostly terrible and our world today is not necessarily as safe—or even as sane—as we are encouraged to believe. Our educational systems begin the brainwashing early, and the structures governing what we must do in order to eat and live in a shelter of some kind are firmly in place. Conform or be homeless and useless to society as we know it. Homelessness in first world countries is rising alarmingly nevertheless. We are encouraged in the pursuit of mindless activities that keep us well away from any thoughts of becoming self-aware individuals, and so we continue to treat our lives with the absolute disregard that we now do. We are born, then most of us are very busy doing things that have little benefit to our souls, the world, or each other, and then we die. What an awful waste. Collectively we have Stockholm Syndrome, but sooner or later something is going to break, because that's what happens to humans when we lie to ourselves for too long. You cannot ever truly lie to yourself indefinitely. We allow our minds and hearts to break rather than accepting the truth that lies in plain sight. But only so much pain can be endured without some kind of uprising. Fortunately that does not have to entail any kind of physical revolution, because clearly a spiritual revolution has already begun around the globe.

Now more and more people are waking up and wanting more, wanting better, wanting change, but change can be painful and confusing. Also, there are a few who have a lot to lose if things change, so they are going to try extremely hard to stop it from happening. Sometimes hard shells have to be broken through for better things to emerge. Hatching may be scary as well as liberating. Even though there are now many who can't see past the broken shells—yet—there are also many who can, and who are very willing to help. These helpers know how very important it is that everyone knows that there are choices to be made, choices that *can* be made, and also that those choices will not be available to make forever. Maybe so many people are awakening at this point in humanity's situation precisely because there is no more time. We are already at a point of no return. If we continue on as we are, the Earth and all who sail on her are going to wish that we had not.

To the understanding of most, no human on this world knows for *certain* what our lives are—what *we* are. We don't know what is really real, what we should be doing with our lives, and if there is some kind of life after death. If there is life after death we don't know what happens there. We don't know what our purpose is or if there even is a purpose to our existence. Are we simply the result of coincidence? Random atoms? What and who are we, and what should we be doing here? Why is life so difficult? Is God real? If He is, why does he allow the terrible evil that goes on in the world? Will the evil be punished when they die? Does it matter? If you knew that you literally could do anything you wanted to do without repercussion, commit murder and inflict pain just because you could, would you?

Strangely, the answer to that last question is usually no. Even without knowing for sure what our lives are all about, people are mostly attracted to good. We don't want to hurt and we don't want to be hurt, but this life—we *believe*—seldom gives us choices. In many ways, all across the globe this appears to be true, but it is not the whole truth. The truth is that there are always choices to be made, even tiny ones, and decisions to be made about ourselves, because what we *know* is *our* truth, and we *know* quite a lot. Life may sometimes be terrifying, but the more we allow ourselves to see and learn, the easier it becomes to see solutions. *We* must decide whether our life is important or not. *We* must decide how we wish to live it. *We* must decide whether we will take action to live it the way we wish to live it, and most of all, *we* must decide whether or not we will stop avoiding viewing our current reality head on.

Have you ever heard anyone say that they were totally happy with the world, themselves, the government, the work they did, and all their life experiences? That they knew where they came from and where they were going? That they approved of or didn't care about war, hatred, cruelty, indifference, starvation, and abuse for any cause or reason, as long as it happened where they didn't have to look at it? It is difficult to say whether or not the people who say these things truly believe them, or if they simply do not want to consider anything too deeply that might cause them pain or discomfort—or more terrifyingly—self-reflection. Things that the knowing of which might force them to take some sort of stand or action against. It is human nature to avoid pain and abuse on a personal level, and the empathetic pain when viewing the suffering of others can hurt very much. And then there are those who get great pleasure from inflicting any kind of evil on any kind of being, who we also avoid looking at. And those others who, like the child who reasons that it would be safer to join the bullies in kicking the dog than to take a chance on the bullies kicking him should he refuse, who both join in evil deeds and encourage them so as not to be ejected from the pack. It is amazing the evil we will allow rather than risk personal discomfort.

Denial and avoidance seldom have happy outcomes, and yet it seems that globally all of humanity is living in a constant state of them. Denial and avoidance of our current realities is the broad path that most of us take in the belief that what we cannot see is not there, and so it can't touch us—or hurt us. We are masters in the art of refusing to look at the possibly painful or frightening aspects of life, and ourselves, but we fail to realise that this refusal to see and accept *what is,* is more damaging to us than not focusing on our realities— the good, the bad, the ugly, the knee meltingly horrendous, or even sometimes the fabulously wonderful, and should be a whole lot more terrifying than seeing what is true. Because the real truth is that refusing to focus on what *is* does *not* make it disappear. It only makes it sink into the recesses of our subconscious, or our collective subconscious—our shadow, where it festers, mutates, and actually grows in power. From there it damages us in multitudes of ways in its inadvertently malicious invisibility. Inadvertent, because the shadow's aim is to protect us, but it is no less destructive because of that blind intent. Frightening as the thought of confronting and focusing on the things that are horrendous in our world or in our memories seems to be, doing just that is the only way to true freedom and joy, and ultimately power over fear.

For those of you who like a little gardening, you will probably at some point have pruned a bush, a plant, or a tree. Ever since my late teens I have had some sort of plant life to tend to. I especially loved roses when I was younger, and in the tiny flat I lived in with my children in my early twenties, I had a small balcony that blazed with colour and fragrance, the space completely filled with large pots containing a wild assortment of rosebushes. These beauties were regularly fertilised, spoken to, and pruned. Each one of them had some of my attention every day. Sometimes a branch would wither and threaten a slow dieback that if ignored could eventually kill the whole plant. A sucker root would push its way up and threaten to overpower a hybrid bush from below. Or an invasion of aphids, or red spider mite, or mould—or any number of outside forces arrived that could cause my bushes to rot away, sicken, or die. It seemed to me that the attempts to hurt, sicken, or kill my fabulous flora were relentless.

The sight of an infected branch, or a leaf covered with fungus or some little sucking creatures did not make me turn away in disgust from a sick plant. It made me spring into action to cut out the infection—or use a spray or tool to help heal it. Then it was up to the rose to work on its recovery. They seldom succumbed, and within a short time a previously half dead looking bush would be thriving, maybe with a hard to see wound, now healed, but still there even though no longer causing pain or threat of death. If I had been too disgusted to look at the rot or invaders, my roses would most certainly have died, or at least not been very happy plants. Just so must you treat your *self*—your inside self and also your outside self. All of the rough and thorny sucker plants and fungus, or biting, devouring, things that surround and hurt your soul begin from outside of you. Look at them. Not looking is the way that monsters can be made. Monsters that grow in the shadows of our world and within ourselves, and sometimes emerge to hurt us and others when we least expect it. Look at them. Before they get any bigger.

Good and evil forces exist on our world. They are real when they murmur on levels that only we are aware of. They are real and tangible in the action or inaction of every human on this planet. Both are trying to get us to pick a side. I believe that the time has come to do just that. For ourselves and for everything and everyone around us. It is time to begin to fix what is broken and leave a better world for those who will come after us.

By sharing what I have learned on the way from being what I thought was broken beyond repair—living a life of unhappiness and no visible purpose—to acceptance, joy, and love, I believe that what I've learned can help others who feel that there is no hope for them. I believe in miracles, because I've lived them. I believe that when we are given much pain, we are also given opportunities to rise from it, and that if we do, we should show others that it is possible for them too.

While recognising that evil is a real and tangible force in our existence, it is very important that while we never like it or appreciate it in any way, we respect it for the damage it can and does do. Never taunt it, think that you can beat it with its own tools of hatred, anger, or fear, and most of all, never underestimate it. Once we know it in all its forms we get to choose whether or not we will allow it in our lives. From there we learn to purposefully select its opposites and finally get to live our lives in joyful freedom.

Jo Robinson
Louis Trichardt, South Africa
October 2019

TABLE OF CONTENTS

PEOPLE ASK QUESTIONS

Many people live lives that, when they think about it, they really don't want to be living. Some manage to convince themselves that they are enjoying these lives. They convince themselves that on the whole humanity is doing alright, and that those times when they get sneaky suspicions that it isn't are the results of something wrong with themselves. When they are struck down with anxiety disorders, Complex Post Traumatic Stress Disorder (C-PTSD), depression or other mental and spiritual ailments, they believe that these things also are the results of something wrong with themselves. When children question the way some things are done we tell them that "that's just the way things are—that's just the way that things are done—the way things have always been done". People learn to accept the way things are and the way things are done, and they try and bury their doubts, their confusion, their guilt and their shame, rather than appear to be different or defective. They do not question anything and attempt not to voice opinions that differ from the mainstream. They see being different as a slippery slope to ridicule and failure. Nobody wants to be an outcast, so people live their lives as best they can according to rules already firmly set in place at their birth by others before them. They keep their opinions to themselves and conform, heads down and blinkers on, and some are quite relieved when the whole life trip comes to an end.

Luckily there are also people who will begin to swim against the tide when they finally look and see what is truth. They'll publicly share their opinions no matter how much these differ from the mainstream. Sometimes they will get shot down or ignored, but at other times many will agree with them. This way many movements have begun which focus on the betterment of our reality. Those that haven't fizzled out are still going strong and gaining ground, however slowly that may be. The problem with forging ahead into new territory is that it's usually not easy. It requires courage, strength and a will to not only focus on personal survival, but the survival of all. It requires a desire to not only improve oneself, but also to take steps, no matter how small, to help others when the truth is that you don't have to.

You don't have to. That is one truth to get properly out of the way first. Ultimately only you are responsible for you. It is your responsibility to act in your own interests without intentionally harming others. You arrive here alone and you leave alone. We almost always have the gift of freedom of choice. And even when we really don't get to choose what we want to do, we always get to choose how we will feel or react in any situation. I must add here that even though I believe that at some point in everyone's life we get to choose who we will be, a word has to be said about those who may never get to that point. Victims of societies that take choices away from their women and girls, or babies born into such poverty that they never get to become toddlers, children struck down by mortal illness or murder, hurt children who have no power to defend themselves from the adults in control of their lives, or victims of abuse so bad that they cannot see a way of escape. Some truly never get to the point of understanding that not only do they get to choose who they become, but that the choices that they make throughout their lives are vitally important. I do believe that those innocents will receive recompense on the other side of their seemingly senseless deaths, but I also believe that nothing is truly senseless, and that good can come of most things, no matter how awful they are when they occur. Even if the terror and torture serves only to show us what we *don't* want. Nothing will show you what *not* to do better than tragedy.

There is much kindness in this world. There are acts of great courage and love to see every day if we look. We must remember that the vast majority of humans are good, with only a small percentage that could be classified as truly bad. Unfortunately many of those are in positions of power. Their decisions impact our very existence, and so we need to work on making things better by understanding that every seemingly small contribution by us will add to the whole, and lead to a mighty force for change when added to all the other single positive actions of others. Earth—beautiful—tragic. The sad thing is that most of the tragic has been brought on by ourselves—humanity. The beautiful thing is that just as humans have shaped the way we now live, the places we live, and even the way our minds and emotions work, humans also have the collective ability to slowly reshape these things away from the darkness that we are clearly heading into. Most of us concentrate on our immediate surroundings. Our family and friends. Where we live and work. Looking further at the hurt that is caused by others, or even indirectly by the way that we live, is painful, so we choose not to consider these things for too long, or at all. After all, what can we as individuals do about war, slavery, terrorism, child abuse, poverty, or the terrible torture of the planet and its creatures?

At various points in human history, certain humans have made *rules* and other humans have accepted them. Many of these now seem to be so ingrained that they could remain forever. We have decided that everything on Earth must have some kind of value according to scales that we have devised. Unless born or promoted to some previously defined elevated state, humans must prove their value by doing work, and thereby justify their right to partake of sustenance, shelter, and other worldly goods. We have in fact extended this to animals. Animals rate according to their value to us. This rating determines how they get to live, how long, or if at all. Humans have taken upon ourselves the right to bestow life or death on everything on this planet according to the value that everything accords us. We have made gods of ourselves, while justifying our collective insanity by using a few paragraphs of the bible to *prove* that God has willed exactly this, or outdated and now proven to be incorrect research as to the sentience of non-humans.

Many people realise this at some level, and some have decided to stop doing it to the best of their abilities. Most go with the flow because that is always easier than making people angry, and there is nothing like feelings of guilt or shame to make people angry. Some people make a lot of money with the way the world works right now, so they will go to great lengths to keep it just as it is for as long as they can. Yet even those people realise that this is not sustainable. Personal gain and personal gratification really can cause actions in people that can destroy a world, and they can and do continue with these actions even with that knowledge. To change will cost them personally and this is more important to them than any cost to any others. They are unlikely to change willingly. At this point humanity has allowed itself to be corralled in ways that seem impossible to get out of. Yet one way or another we will have to get out. The question is will we get out in time?

Why are we here? None of us know beyond doubt, and there are some pretty kooky theories out there, so it's not your usual dinner party discussion. There have been great men and women who have tried to find out, but there is no actual definitive list anywhere that we can see that tells us what the point of *us* is, or what we should be doing and striving towards, if there is anything to be doing and striving towards at all. Some believe in one Creator of everything, or that we are ourselves co-creating everything including ourselves. Some believe in God the Father and Jesus Christ the Son. Some have a multitude of gods and demigods. Some people believe in God but scoff at the idea of the devil. Some make the devil their god and believe even so that their afterlife will be fabulous in Hell. Others believe in randomness and lucky connections between atoms, and that this is all there is. That when you die you're dead and there is no purpose involved in our lives at all. Some take this even further and say that life is all about your own pleasure, and that you can do anything, no matter how terrible, and there will be no payback. Some say that whatever you believe is your truth. If you believe in biblical Heaven and Hell then you will go to one of them when you expire here. If you believe that there is no punishment for mass murder, and that you will die to find yourself in the midst of a bevy of nubile virgins, then so be it. I would imagine that that kind of heaven would become a hell quite soon once the novelty wears off and the young ladies get to chatting amongst themselves.

Throughout human history people have tried to make sense of our reason to exist as we do with various religions and dogmas. What is interesting is that the majority of them have one main thing to say at their cores—that love is the most important thing that there is. They mostly all point us in the direction of being and doing good, even though over time quite a lot of their messages have become rather twisted out of shape. Some people have claimed to have seen some aspect of the afterlife or Heaven after a near death experience. Many of these seem extremely credible, medically speaking, and while not all have had exactly the same experiences they are remarkably similar. Naysayers will say (scientifically truthfully) that every cell in the human body doesn't die at the official time of death, so maybe these people's physical consciousnesses are somehow still in bits of their bodies that aren't quite dead yet, dreaming what they believe. Unless you have such an experience yourself you can never know the truth of the experiences of others, so you have to make your own choices about what to believe without much concrete evidence.

Most of us don't think about death until we come face to face with it, as we all do with family, friends, and pets—and of course ultimately at the end of our own lives unless we exit early in some sudden and unexpected way. We avoid thinking about death unless we have to, and when we do, we generally think of it with fear. Sooner or later we must think about death, but by then for most of us it is too late to use the fact of the inevitability of it to change the way we live. The truth is that honestly considering the reality that we have a finite time to live on Earth can indeed change the way that we think and so lead us to begin to live the best life that we can, for ourselves and others, regardless of what happens afterwards.

Do you believe in life after death? There are people on both sides of this fence and there are very many variations of beliefs about what happens once we depart this mortal coil. Whether or not you believe can shape the way you live. If you believe that your death will be the end of you entirely, then it might not matter very much to you how you live. If you believe in reincarnation the same can apply if you think that you have limitless do-over lives to correct any mistakes in this life. If you believe in a kind and loving God, it can be difficult to understand why some people don't seem to have the mental acuity to live good lives if they only one shot at it. If you believe in a vengeful God you could spend your time being very strict and hard on yourself and others in your environment. On the other side of that coin there are those who twist the verses in the Bible and convince themselves that it doesn't matter what they do because if they say sorry any and all sins will be forgiven. That seems a slippery slope to me. The idea, I think, is to live the best life you can regardless of the outcome simply because if you do you will enjoy the journey, and even if that's all you're going to get it is much better than living a life immersed in pain, worry, or anger.

I've read a lot of books on my journey to understand why we exist and what the point is of it all. Some of them seemed to have all the answers. A lot of them told me that I am the creator—that we are all creating our own reality while we are here while being a part of a universal oneness. This is true in a large part, but believing this verbatim can lead to a very lonely feeling. It sounds like quite a job, and a little hard to understand, being the creator of everything while incarnated on Earth and then possibly merging into some sort of collective and distinctly un-individual perfect consciousness of everything when we die, only to have to start all over again and again, forever. I personally have had too many mind-blowing experiences that most certainly were not created by me to completely embrace this idea, so I try to be open-minded about all possibilities. The truth is that we don't know anything other than what we can personally see and what we *know* that we feel because of that seeing. What I now do know is that are never alone. We have guidance and help from a good source, that while ethereal, is nonetheless able to be felt. We have goading and temptation also from some equally real malignant force. Good and evil are both out there building their teams in this world, and you deny both or either one of them their actual existence at your peril.

We are all free to choose, but it's always interesting to see what others think because you never know what you will learn that way. It is never a good idea to try and force belief on anyone. I don't wish to do that at all, even though I hope to encourage people to face all of their reality, because that will indeed make lives better. I've changed my own mind often enough. Until not very long ago I was a staunch believer in The Universe and the Law of Attraction and I ran away speedily from anyone who looked like they were about to begin spouting verses at me. My superpowers have always been logic and a leaning towards the scientific—if I can't see it, I don't believe it. I'm still that way. I've just changed my understanding of what seeing is. I wasn't raised as a churchgoer—about as far from that as you can get in fact. God, angels, and devils were not part of my world, even though I could not deny the existence of ghosts, having seen a couple of those for myself. But I'd never seen God—I'd never seen an angel— and thankfully I'd never seen a devil, so I never really believed in them—until I realised that the *results* of the existence of good and evil were *everywhere*. Those I could see quite clearly. Therefore they are indeed to be believed in, whatever we choose to call them.

Now I certainly know that there is something helping me. Something loving, wise, and kind. Something that has always been with me no matter how stupid or illogically I was behaving at the time. I don't know what this something's name is or what form it takes, or whether or not it takes a physical form at all. For lack of this knowledge I find it easier to call this force God. This force stepped into my life in such a way that I could not hold on to my previous disbelief, negativity, and fear. This force certainly made a huge and loving presence known to me in the most impossible ways, and with such meticulous attention to detail of the things that I needed that I could not logically cling to my disbelief.

Evil is an actual force in this world. A force that wants us to fail, to fear, to harm. It is really good at what it does, and its greatest weapon is our insistence in not believing in it. Feeling love is much more enjoyable than feeling any of love's opposites, and yet people consistently choose the unpleasant things. If we are constantly immersed in rage, hatred and fear, and consistently acting from these feelings, there may well come a point where we can indeed find ourselves completely apart from good—from God. Why would anyone even consider taking such a chance? Critical mass must be reached for one side or the other, and if the majority of your choices are evil, well then—

Evil cannot exist where good exists and there are *always* consequences for the enactment of one or the other. The whole course of every human life is about making choices, and every choice that we make has an effect either on others or ourselves, or both. Our choices shape who we are as well as the world around us. We get to choose whether or not to believe that our individual lives have purpose or not. If we look around us it seems that the obvious purpose is to choose sides. How we deal with challenges defines what we become spiritually in the end. We have to choose sides, and once we tip the balance within us and without us one way or another, we get to live with our choices. Obviously there are other purposes in individual lives, and we have our callings, whether they be small or large in our eyes, and with those we get to fight for our chosen camps. We interact with others and influence them with our behaviours, words, and deeds, but at the bottom of it all are choices—our freely made choices to go with darkness or light.

Good is real. You can see it in many things. Evil is real. You can see it in many things. From the resistance that causes you to procrastinate rather than create the masterpiece you desperately want to create, to the bomb going off in the middle of a crowded place of innocents. The child helping a beggar to his feet after an embarrassing fall, or the big gruff man gently helping a baby bird back into its nest. If there is any point to life at all it has to be to be to choose between good and evil. We have help and guidance from both teams, but ultimately the choice will be ours. We have to accept that learning is a continuous process. Our current reality is such that there are no miracle revelations for us to find to completely fix every part of our lives. When we learn one thing we move on to the next lesson. We have to *choose* to live our best lives—or not.

Nobody knows and can prove beyond doubt whether this life is a one shot deal, or whether reincarnation is they way of things, but there is enough hard science now to support the fact that our consciousness is not our brain. There is enough evidence to show that consciousness animates our bodies and departs when our bodies die. Simply not believing that you are a soul that will continue on when your body stops cannot extinguish that soul, although that belief can possibly create problems for yourself moving smoothly onwards when the time comes. But even if such an awful thing was true—that when you die here you're gone in every way forever—why not live a good life anyway? Why not make your mark here and leave this world with memories of your good choices rather than leaving a trail of wounding and uncaring? It can't hurt, and when you realise that you really do have the freedom to choose good, life becomes a lot easier to live. Because that's when the support will come in amazing ways and you'll realise after all that there is a lot more to this whole deal, and that *you* do indeed matter in the great scheme of things in a very important way.

Every single good choice made when an evil one looks easier or appears more attractive in some way is another notch in the team belt. They all count no matter how insignificant you may think that little old you and your choices are. The opposite is true. Not one soul is insignificant. Often the most powerful warriors are the ones nobody sees, and small secret kindnesses cause the mightiest ripples in that unseen world around us where both sides hang out cheering us on one way or another.

Forrest Gump said "Life is like is like a box of chocolates. You never know what you're gonna get". I prefer to think of life like a game of cards. Many times you're dealt a rotten hand—a hand that makes it appear that you have no chance at all of winning. Then you put on that old poker face, and you pick up your three new cards after tossing the worst of the first away, and you end up with four aces. There is no point in throwing the hand you were dealt into the centre of the table, trying to slap the dealer, and then hiding out under the table, hating him and feeling sorry for yourself until the game is over.

Even if the dealer really doesn't like you, or doesn't care one way or another about you, but simply cheated so that he would be assured of the win at your expense, what benefit is there to you in giving up? You then just help that crook to acquire his ill-gotten gains while at the same time making yourself ill with rage and self-pity. Sometimes you will win and sometimes you won't, but you can choose to enjoy the whole game no matter how many hands you win, in the knowledge that you did your best.

Have you ever watched the television show called Chopped? Four contestants get three timed rounds of cooking with set ingredients. The ingredients are chosen randomly. They mostly don't seem to go with each other at all, and some of them are just plain disgusting. The contestants are also unique—with their own characters, talents, experience and abilities. They have different levels of self-control, and few of them aren't obviously stressed. But there is always a winner, and often these people create delicious and beautiful plates of food with things that most of us would immediately consign to the trash. Why? Because even while their fear is very real, they relegate it to the back burner while they're competing. They concentrate on what they do have, not worrying about what they don't have, and they use discipline to use the abilities and knowledge that they do have to do the best that they can with those mismatched ingredients.

Chopped is like a condensed version of all of our lives. Sometimes the ingredients at the beginning of the show are perfect—delicious—well matched. There are always losers even so, even with all the benefits possible. Sometimes the contestants look very much like losers out of the starting gates, with ingredients that seem to predict awful results. But the human spirit is a powerful thing when tapped and worked with. No matter how bad your ingredients are to begin with, you will always be a wildcard, and the absolute truth is that only you get to decide how fabulous your final dish will be. It is not always easy, but there is a wonderful thing that only those who do strive find out. The minute you make the decision and take the first step, there are awesome powers out there that will step in and give you miracles. Take who you are, no matter how disadvantaged you might think that you are, and mix in those ingredients, no matter how substandard they may appear to be, and take your best shot. Why not? What have you got to lose?

Too many people allow the beliefs and opinions of others about them to influence what they do or how they behave. They worry about what others will think about them, or what they will say or do. This really should not matter to you—whether you love or don't care much for these others—either way it does not matter what they think or say to or about you. They will not be there when your life is over, and you finally figure out the true meaning of it all. They will not be there when you become more self-aware, and they will not be there as you learn and grow through your pain, tribulations, and striving. No matter how silly others think that you look, their opinions and beliefs don't count. When it comes to living your life, only *yours* do. Always follow the beat of your own drum. You are the *only* one accountable, and only your own actions count.

Regardless of what anyone says or does to you, no matter how awful or wonderful, only your decisions, thoughts, and actions count in your life, and no matter how badly the deck seems to be stacked against you, you can still choose to make decisions that can make *you* better. Find what *you* believe and live according to that. It is the most important thing to you and also to the world around you.

PEOPLE PREFER CAKE

Hope and faith in the face of incredibly impossible to overcome challenges is truly amazing in sentient creatures, especially humans. Even when success is pretty much guaranteed not to happen, there is usually a tiny flicker of hope in a last minute miracle. We are inspired and fired up when we read or hear about those very, very few people who become millionaires after overcoming outrageous pain and hardship. We marvel at miraculous healings, near misses and divine interventions. We always have a belief, no matter how miniscule, that we could maybe be on the receiving end of things like this too. Honestly though, of all the people you have ever known, how many of them achieved absolute happiness? How many of them beat their illnesses against all odds? How many of them achieved financial or other success while doing what made them blissfully happy? Mostly life is what it is. Hard work will generally pay off in some way—big or small—while relying on miracles while gazing at stars without doing any work at all will probably end in sleeping under the stars.

I am a firm believer in miracles—don't get me wrong. I am not saying that hope and faith are not to be cultivated. They are essential in our lives, and I personally have seen many, many miracles. The thing is that sometimes a perfect outcome is actually to be found in failure. We will never learn a thing if we never fall down. If we never learn what pain feels like we will never learn how not to inflict it. If we are never humiliated we will never know what another feels like when we unknowingly humiliate them. We will never understand freedom if we are never trapped. We will never know courage if we never feel fear. We will never truly know love unless we have experienced no love. Rather than losing hope and faith when we are hurt, we must learn to have faith that no matter what the outcomes are, we always have the choice to emerge better. We must learn to have faith that even though those forces for good that surround us are not enjoying standing back and allowing us to suffer, they have faith that we will indeed learn from these things and become better and stronger because of them. It is also good to understand that we were designed to strive. It is in our DNA to want to create, to solve, to overcome. We must learn to always take first steps no matter how fearful they look.

Not many people are seekers of pain. Most will go to some lengths to avoid it if at all possible. None of us get through life without sometimes being hurt and at other times experiencing great joy. You don't have to have been abused in any way at all to have experienced pain at a level enough to cause physical, emotional, or spiritual damage. Some people seem to get more than their fair share while others seem to sail through their lives without much at all. Some people start accumulating their pain right out of the starting gates at birth, and carry on collecting it right up until the day that they die. Others seem to have mostly joy, fun, love, and laughter for their entire trips. It can make you wonder if everything really is random when you see the terrible traumatic lives some wonderfully good and kind people endure while nasty evildoers live lives of opulence and abundance. But it can also greatly inspire you when you see that pain can actually make you a better person, and possibly the greater the hardships you successfully deal with here on Earth, the greater the benefits to your enduring soul.

One thing is clear. Nobody leads an always perfectly happy, joy-filled life. Also clear is that nobody is meant to. It's hard to understand and accept that is in the moments of our greatest suffering that we can have the greatest breakthroughs. Pain can make us grow, and make us heal. When we run from pain and fight it, we can end up bitter, miserable, and occasionally just plain mean. When we face it and walk through it in the knowledge that pain isn't forever—when we hold on to whatever courage we can muster and try to find the lessons that are in it—*and there are always lessons in pain*—we find out things about ourselves that we never realised before its onset. We unearth deep wounds that could have been hurting us for our whole lives without us realising it. We find that walking through the pain can help us understand and heal these wounds. Going through our sufferings with our eyes wide open, living through whatever inner agony they bring, just like when a broken bone heals stronger around the break than it was before, so our souls can find greater strength when a wound has healed.

Pain is horrible, and there are different levels of it, just as there are different levels of joy. It is easy to take joy for granted when it's your normal, but pain is very difficult to ignore. Some do manage to mostly ignore it, but that is a very dangerous thing to have accomplished. Because the pain isn't gone, it's just buried. It's still going to impact your life while it is buried without being addressed, and it is going to hurt just as much when you unearth it years later, as you must eventually do if you want to heal. So the sooner you work through it the better. The only way to heal pain is to go through it. Just as with fear, it has to be overcome by being seen, felt, and gone through. One of the most amazing benefits of working through your pain is that afterwards you will find that you can reach new heights of joy. New levels of empathy and gratitude. Just as a rough hunk of ore will go through the flames and be tempered before becoming a beautiful silver cup, so can we be tempered by the pains we encounter throughout our lives. It all depends on whether or not you are prepared to feel your pain when it happens, and then move on from it. Once it is done you won't ever feel it at its maximum again—you might get a twinge now and then, but once you've actually lived through it, truly felt it, future new pains will be much easier to deal with. You have to learn to leave them behind you, not within you.

It is sad to say that in many respects in this world today it appears that we don't have the freedom or ability to choose what we truly desire. In oppressed nations under the domination of despots any sort of personal freedom is a rarity. In the Western world also there are some things that we have little or no power to change. Humans often prefer to believe that they don't have freedom of choice, even though they really have no desire to have to choose in certain circumstances. This sometimes allows us to do things that we aren't entirely comfortable with and not have to take responsibility for doing it. Others made those choices for us. The government. Our parents. Our cultures. Even if there is a small voice within us that consistently tells us that a certain action is wrong, we allow ourselves to continue to do it because everyone else does. So it must be right. Right?

Most of us use the *everyone else does* it free ticket at some point or another to do something that we like to do even though we believe that we shouldn't. We can see things that we deeply feel are wrong to do, and yet we still choose to partake simply because it's easy to do so. Often we will even speak out against others who voice our own niggling beliefs of the wrongness of doing something simply to prevent ourselves being seen by our tribe as going against established norms. Swimming against the tide can make you a pariah in your social or family circles. Modern living has become very busy, and most of our waking lives are stuffed with things that we believe must be done. Mostly we don't take time to stop and consider the choices we are making. We continue in the ways that we have been shown by our parents, caregivers, peers, and those who govern us and this world in one way or another. We teach and show our children these same things. We continue to do things that we *know* inside are not right and maintain this legacy onwards through our offspring.

That sense of *knowing* has often led to sinking feelings in my life. I am not ashamed to say that just as we all have, during the course of my life I have more often than I like to admit pushed those nudges firmly away—sent them back down to whatever part within me they rose up from—and made the choices I was not comfortable making simply to keep the peace. I've learned now that it is ultimately better for ourselves when we do make the choices that we *know* are the best for ourselves, regardless of the outcomes. It is not easy. We are human and nobody can say that being human is easy. Most of us don't like to take on what is hard when easy is a choice that will not only not get you into trouble, but is a choice that *everyone else* makes all the time.

These choices can be made as the fleeting knowledge that what you are about to eat has been heinously treated arises and eating it anyway, or as actually choosing to physically, emotionally, or verbally harm another *or yourself* directly. It can be choosing to hold on to victimhood, or the instilled belief that you are bad or of no value because someone else has told you so. It can be choosing to hurt others because you have been hurt. It can be watching those in power do things that you know are evil, and yet choosing not to add your voice to those who are trying to stop them. There will always be those of us who choose to stick our necks out, and that is good. It is amazing what a million signatures made up of single choices can do. Even if they accomplish nothing, at least you will have acted in honour of your own truth of what you *know* to be wrong for you or others. If you feel nothing, then that is fine for you too. Freedom of choice is about what is wrong or right for *you*. Those little knowing feelings will always make themselves felt—no matter how briefly. Respect yourself by allowing them in and considering your actions before you ignore them. Sometimes the painful or unpopular choices are best after all.

This can be harder for some, but still it is something to strive for. Those who have had formative years where they were not loved unconditionally and allowed to form their own opinions, but rather were shown that if they didn't make the choices expected of them they would be punished in one way or another, can find that voicing what they truly believe is more difficult than for those who were gently and kindly nurtured. They have been taught that they are worth less than others, and that their ideas and beliefs are not even remotely as important as anyone else's. They sometimes find themselves stuck this way for their entire lifetimes. They constantly stuff their sense of right and wrong, and their entitlement to live their own lives as they choose, deep down to the shadowy recesses within themselves. When these particular people do finally realise that they can, and should, make their own choices and find their voices, they can be some of the most powerful and inspiring voices of all.

We really do get to choose how we feel. It is not easy to break the ingrained habits of a lifetime. We must try. We must learn to always be able to exercise our freedom to choose both what we do and how we feel. We must learn that it is not selfish, but self-respecting, and that it is hugely important take full responsibility for ourselves. Even if current circumstances seem horrendous and impossible to escape from. Especially then. These choices may involve the difficult path of truly moving on from various forms of childhood or adult abuse rather than *choosing* to allow these things to continue to poison our lives. It is a choice to live in anger, self-pity, and self-destruction as a continuation of past or even current abuse. It is also choice to let go of these things and move forward positively with love and care. This choice will never turn out worse than the choice of *deciding* to stay in an evil cycle. Choice is always an option no matter how terrible circumstances seem, even if the choice is simply to choose how we feel and who we will become.

PEOPLE WONDER WHAT THEY ARE

What is real? Are you real? Who are you? Sometimes we spend so much time trying to be someone else that we seldom allow ourselves to fully experience who we actually are. We try to be what others expect us to be, and we project personas that aren't at all who we really are. Mostly we would never dream of revealing what we truly think and feel when negative emotions rise. When certain characteristics of our real selves try to surface we push them down because we're afraid that these parts of who we are will be unacceptable, offensive, laughable, or ridiculous to the people whose opinions are important to us. These opinions are often more important to us than our own. And so we stifle parts of our personality. This is never good for anyone's mental health and emotional wellbeing, because our personality as a whole is who we are. Who we are includes those aspects of ourselves that we dislike or are ashamed of.

Occasionally we will come across one of those rare creatures we condescendingly label a free spirit. Our admiration of their originality is tempered with a slightly smug gratitude for our own normality. And yet a common deathbed regret is one of not having allowed yourself to be who you really are—to live a genuine life—because at that point, when all the fluff of this life is no longer relevant and you realise that's there is no way to retreat from the departure lounge, you finally get it that there is no more important thing in life than to *be you* through all of it. When it's too late to begin your journey to living as your authentic self you realise that it might not have been such an impossible and terrifying trip to have taken after all. You realise that it should have been much more important than scaling the corporate ladder, keeping up with the Joneses, or pretending to be someone that society expected you to be whether you liked that someone or not.

We are all made up of many parts, many of which we are not consciously aware of unless we choose to travel inwardly. When we find ourselves hurting—when we decide that we want more from our lives, and when we want to know *who* we actually are underneath all our crazy, tumultuous waking thoughts and impulses, we find that we must undertake a journey to find all of these parts so that we can knit them together before we can truly understand our whole selves. It's quite a trip, full of surprises, some of them not pleasant, but the further along the road we travel, the more joy we find as we meet more of ourselves. As we connect all the pieces of who we are, warts and all, it's impossible for love not to grow in every direction—inward and outward.

When it comes to hurting ourselves we lose sight of the fact that we are our only true protector. We might like to think that we love ourselves but often this is not the case. We usually have beliefs that we should be better in some way or another. Or that we should not be the way we are. Should seems like such an innocuous word, but in truth it is a sharp knife that we can use to stab ourselves in the centre of who we really are over and over again, day after day, for the whole of our lives. We also tell ourselves that we are stupid, useless, lazy, ugly, uneducated, unworthy, and many more horrible things that we would never dream of uttering out loud to anyone that we don't particularly care about one way or another, let alone to someone who we love. We don't love ourselves because we don't know and accept who we are. Who we are is buried under so many layers of shoulds and insults that we mostly don't know that we are any different underneath. But we are there, and the most important work any of us has to do in this life is to find our true selves, and once we do, to love ourselves.

Let's look at a couple of examples of what we really want and what we are taught to believe that we should want. How about a pair of young siblings? The girl, Susan, wants to be an archaeologist when she grows up. She spends all her free time examining rocks and pot shards, and can't get enough reading of books about prehistory and the amazing discoveries archaeologists have made. Her brother Alan only wants to draw and paint—he wants to be an artist. Unfortunately their parents can't afford to send Susan to university and Alan to art school. The young pair are quickly taught that their wanting such things is not only unrealistic but selfish. What they should be wanting is to get "real" jobs as soon as possible and begin to earn their way properly in this world. When rebellious feelings arise—when they find themselves hating the work that they find to do to support themselves—these feelings are quickly replaced with guilt. How selfish to *want* to paint all day. How selfish to *want* to discover buried treasures.

Alan finds work as a clerk. Eventually he works his way up to office manager. He never draws or paints again. He marries and has two children. He teaches them not to be greedy and expect things that he can't afford to give them. Alan goes to his job every day. On weekends he mows his lawn and watches television. He retires. He dies. He never experiences the joy of doing what he really wants to do, and he believes that that is right. If he was good enough to do what he wanted he would have been born with the resources to do so after all. Something about *who he is* must be wrong. Susan hasn't considered whether or not she wants to be married and have a family, but an overzealous date and her innate inability to say no to the wants of others finds her pregnant at the age of 18. She does know that she could never kill anything on purpose so abortion is out of the question. She has been taught that being single and pregnant at such a young age is something to be very ashamed of. She is now taught that she has brought this on herself due to her own bad behaviour and so she must deal with the consequences. She doesn't want to be a mother or a wife, but she now believes that she should want to be a mother because the people around her say so. She gets married and her baby is born. She does not enjoy either process, but she knows that she should—she also now knows that there must be *something deeply wrong with her* for not wanting these things. She pretends. Everyone thinks what a great mom and homemaker she is, but she knows the truth. At her core she knows that she is defective for wanting other things. Over the years Susan learns that her true wants are selfish, and that she should be grateful for the things she has.

We feel guilty for wanting to buy a bottle of wine and drink it while doing nothing at all when we know that we should rather want to pay bills and soberly clean our home. We feel guilty when we become angry or irritated at friends or family when we know we should be loving towards them. We feel guilty when we sit at our desk at work hating being there with every cell in our body when we know we should be grateful to have a wage at the end of each month. These shameful knowings do not go away by themselves. Sometimes they gang up and have us believing that we ourselves are shameful things entirely. We have to knowingly spend some time with them and realise that there is no shame at all in wanting anything. Different societies have varying things to shame us with. These levels of shame and self-loathing can be built up to the point where we consistently punish ourselves in a whole lot of genius ways to ensure that we never succeed at much and stay pretty miserable. We procrastinate when we could be working towards doing something that we love. We self-sabotage. We punish ourselves for being ourselves. This seems to be becoming the norm in our current society, but it is something we must consciously and actively stop doing. You are allowed to want anything at all, and you are allowed to do whatever you can to get it without anyone telling you that you do not deserve it.

Compassion and acceptance of who you are will be the seeds that grow into love. When you realise that perfection is not normal for anyone anywhere, and that your blemishes and spiritual scars did not come about because you are inherently bad. When you realise that you are allowed to be human you can begin to heal the things about yourself that you want to change with affection and kindness. When you have those things for yourself, you will be amazed to find that they begin to arrive for others, even others who don't at first sight appear to be at all loveable or deserving of compassion. The key to life, and the answer to all our questions lies with love, and by loving ourselves first and foremost. You need to know who you are if you are to love who you are, and even though the destination is the most wonderful thing, the journey to finding your true self can be painful. Even so, you it will always be worth it.

We carry with us a surprising amount of who we are not. Consciously or subconsciously we believe that we are any number of pretty rotten things, and when desperate little reminders try to pop up of the wonderful things we are, we do the mental equivalent of knocking them on their heads with a hammer. We are taught that loving ourselves is selfish and wrong, and when we see the damage that is done by those who love themselves *too much* and at the expense of all else, we dig our mental heels in further. We don't want to be like that. We are equally fervent in our desire not to be hurt. So we try to let our love flow only outwards, or we lock it away entirely to prevent ourselves being made vulnerable because of it, and thereby open ourselves up to the probability of even more pain down the road.

To completely avoid pain during the course of our lives is impossible. There is a point to pain. It is necessary for growth. Still—we want none of it. We do all sorts of things to try and bypass or ignore it, and we cause pain to who we really are with these attempts. It is painful to believe that we are bad in any way. We choose not to acknowledge any parts of ourselves that we believe to be bad, whether this is true or not. Many of us are unconscious perfectionists, and we believe that if we acknowledge and accept anything *bad* about ourselves we are allowing ourselves to actually *be* bad, or accepting that we already *are* intrinsically bad. There is not one single person who has not buried something about themselves that they feel is unworthy or bad so deeply that they believe that they have cut it off from who they really are. You can't do that. You can only pretend that it is not a part of who you are, or who you think you were.

Realising that these buried pieces are all part of you, even those you believe to be bad, and that they have to be brought up to your consciousness and integrated, can be a major sticking point to beginning to truly know and yet still love yourself. It is important to understand that while you don't have to like all the things that you have done, or all the negative impulses that rise in you, you can learn to view yourself with compassion and acceptance anyway, and realise that these things only confirm that you are human. You are here to learn. Perfection is not expected of you. You are here to choose sides. You will fail and you will fall, and that is perfect. You are perfectly imperfect, and in *recognising* those times when you have been imperfect and trying never to repeat them—rather than ignoring them and pretending they never happened—makes you very loveable indeed.

You will learn nothing of importance without understanding what is important to you. Once you realise that you have done something wrong, or even something terribly wrong, and it makes you feel such remorse, guilt, or shame that those feelings seem like more than you can bear, you must also understand that burying these feelings will only lead to an exclusion of a part of yourself. You must own, and you must love all of who you are, even those parts that you see as bad or ugly—those parts that really did do something terrible. There are some people who do get joy from hurting others, but that is not the case with most of us, and the things that we sometimes do that have awful outcomes for ourselves or others are seldom done with malice or intent. So while we know that we would never create another scenario like the one that caused harm, we can learn to appreciate the lesson that we learned from it without punishing ourselves for the rest of our lives. We can accept our fallibility and learn to love ourselves while realising that while we are not perfect, we are still deserving of our own love at the very least.

You are no more or less entitled to a wonderful life than anyone else. It doesn't matter where you were born, or to what family. Your shape, colour, and gender have no relevance. All of these things, as well as what has been done to you, and what you have done for good or bad, right up until this very moment can only have power over you if you allow it. We can't change what is, and we can't change the past. We can only learn from it and refuse to allow it to harm us anymore. Then we get to change our future.

Before you begin your journey to you, and before you dive within to stir up all the shadows in you that have been buried so deep you've forgotten that they exist, you have to make a promise to yourself that you will not allow yourself to be angry with yourself. No matter what you did or caused to happen at any point in your life, decide now that you will view these things as if you were viewing them in someone other than yourself. Someone who you love already. Take notes and delve into the reasons for acting the way that you did. This is not to excuse the actions, but only to understand them better. Mostly you will find that the things we do that shame us, and that we bury, we usually do from fear. Fear can bring anger, terror, and powerful instincts of self-preservation to the fore, justified or not. Regardless of how spiritual and perfect we may feel we should be, we are nevertheless installed in a body designed just like any animal, full of chemical signals and instincts that rise in the face of outside threats or challenges. Sometimes thinking just doesn't happen in time to stop a disaster. Would you not have compassion for someone who you dearly love who does something bad when they are overcome by these things? Of course you would. Once you find the true reasons behind bad actions you will find that you don't actually have to hate yourself because of them, and so you can accept those parts of yourself back into the wholeness that you should be. A wonderful side-effect of this is that much compassion comes for those who have hurt us when we understand our own very real capacity to hurt others, and still accept who we are with love.

Luckily not all that is buried within you is not going to be painful to dig out. We bury some fantastic joys and talents also. While viewing yourself with compassion, you will realise that it is perfectly alright to love things that might now seem silly to others, not profitable, or childish, and not only is it alright to love them, it is vital to bring them up and allow them to be part of who you are once again. Remember—you can never totally remove anything that has ever been part of who you are, no matter how briefly. Once you acknowledge the parts of you that you have been ashamed of in one way or another, and accept and integrate these things into the wholeness of who you are now, you don't have to wallow in them. You don't have to think about them, and indeed you must not go over them other than to understand and accept them before letting thoughts of them go. Don't give too much thinking time to evil—ever. The fabulous bits that come up though—*do* wallow in these just as much as you like. Act on these things. Draw silly pictures—swing in the park—sing, play, dance, recite poetry, make a gingerbread house just as big as you like. Surround yourself with what you love. Buy yourself the present you always wanted but never got, even if it's a toy your parents couldn't afford when you were five. Buy it—play with it—enjoy being with that part of you that you now love enjoying that wanted thing, no matter how silly it seems to anyone else.

The first thing to remember about who you are is that *you* are more important to *you* than you realise. Nothing is more important to you than you are. That is an odd sounding sentence, but do give it some thought. *Nothing is more important to you than you.* Many people get a little cranky when anyone says something like "We are born alone and we will die alone" because they think that's a morbid and scary thought. Of course we are with our parents when we are born, and hopefully our deathbeds will be surrounded by those who love us, there to see us on our way to our next incarnation. If you think about it though, the journey of the soul into this world and out of it again is done only by the soul. No matter what happens during the course of our lives, the only thing that truly matters to our soul is what we take from the journey. What we learn, who we love, the good things that we do and leave behind—even the bad things that we do that teach others not to do those same things. We start out as one personality and our lives change that personality to who we are when we die. Our choices tilt the scales—good or bad—and we don't leave the same as we were when we arrived.

We all have free will, and some people consistently choose to enjoy themselves in the physical world regardless of the consequences, even though they are fully aware that those consequences are detrimental, hurtful, or dangerous to themselves or others. Sometimes they get pleasure from these consequences—they enjoy watching others being hurt or failing, because it makes them feel superior. These consistent choices throughout their lives change who they arrived as, and when they leave they will have become more *consciously* evil beings. Don't believe that when you die your soul automatically shakes off all the evil that you have *chosen* to do with the *knowledge* that it is evil. You are a consciousness that is always growing. If you choose to consistently make bad choices with full awareness that these choices are evil, then you choose to make the dark things part of *who you are*, and you bury and stifle the potential for good that we are all born with. You will take that with you on your journey further on after this life, just as if you choose to grow your goodness—to make it bigger—you will take that with you as part of who you are too.

All of life is choices. Nothing can change who you choose to become— who you really are—unless you let it. You always have choice. We abdicate our right to choose sometimes because we allow ourselves to believe that we actually don't have a choice. While that is never the truth it becomes true for us for as long as we choose not to recognise our own power. We think that we will never amount to anything because we are lacking in something—education, money, talent, looks, lovability, courage. We believe that the things done to us by others have changed or damaged us in ways that we cannot overcome. We give our power to others when we believe that someone else has to do all the work to fix us. In this instance we choose to believe that we have no power at all. While it is true that we do need help throughout our lives from those powerful forces of good or evil that will help us to get what we choose, we forget that we have to play our part also. You can't sit around and wait for God to make you take the first step to doing something that scares you—*you are the one that has to move your foot*. No evil force can physically force you to kick a puppy. Once again you have to move your foot. There are no magic pills to instantly make you into what you want to be but don't believe that you can be. Only you can do that. But—big but— that doesn't have to be as scary as it could be. You have huge strength within you if you choose to call on it. The who that you truly are is more powerful than you might realise.

You are unique. There is no other you anywhere in the universe. The you that you are today is nothing at all like the you that you were twenty years ago. Physically, mentally, spiritually, you are completely one of a kind right now, just as you will be completely different from what you are now in a year, or a month, or a decade from now. There are more than fifty trillion cells in your body and every single one of them dies off regularly and is replaced with a completely new one, *except* for your brain cells. When a neuron dies in your cerebral cortex it is not replaced, so we should try and keep the old grey matter as healthy as we can with mental exercise and physical habits that don't kill them off sooner than necessary. There's a popular saying that your body is completely renewed every seven years, and while apart from the brain cells, this is true, your cells actually die off and are replaced every couple of days or weeks, depending on the type of cell. Our mental activity reflects in our body and vice versa. What we believe manifests in our bodies in many ways, and once something gets going in our bodies it can affect us mentally and emotionally.

Figuring out who we really are isn't easy. Where is the actual you? Our thoughts seem to be situated in our heads but our feelings seem to emanate from our middle sections. Where do our thoughts come from? We all have some doozies of thoughts, don't we? Are these really our own thoughts beginning somewhere inside us—in our brains—or do they originate somewhere outside of us? What separates body, mind, and soul? Are they different entities or are they really all the same thing? How about the psychiatric tool of inner child work—where you identify a child (or several children) within you—that child being you, but not a part of you that you're consciously aware of—just at some younger stage of arrested development—and talk directly to him or her so that he or she can heal and move on. How many people are in there, you wonder? How disturbing to think that there are multiple yous inside of you that you are not aware of. What else could be lurking in inside of you? Some things can be downright terrifying when you really get into them, and it's not hard to see why not many people are prepared to sit down all alone with themselves and go and have an actual look at their interior landscapes.

You must learn to never be afraid of yourself, or any particular part of yourself. To do this you must learn to know yourself. When you see that all your "inner children" went into hiding because something made them fearful, and when you understand that while you are not consciously aware or them, they are still working within you to "protect" you from what sent them into hiding in the first place. What they (you at the time) perceived as a threat to their existence is probably not something that is good for you to be afraid of right now. These terrified mini-yous could very well be filling you with fear when you consider taking a step towards success, independence or happiness, and freezing you in your tracks when you have something important to you that needs to be done. When you do seek out and find these little bits of you, and understand the reasons for their fear, you will be filled with compassion for these previous incarnations of yourself, and you will do the work that you need to do to help them understand that they no longer need to be afraid. One by one you thereby integrate another broken off piece into the whole that is you. Not only will this release you from those nebulous fears that seem to come from nowhere and knobble your chances of success, but *you* will now be bigger, and further along on your journey to conscious wholeness. It's amazing how truly strong and courageous you find out that you have actually been all along when you feel the desire to heal and protect these children that are you. And heal them you can.

You need to have a *you* to experience anything, because unless you do nothing will have any particular meaning. Your reaction to anything that happens in life purely has to do with *you*. Even if you believe that you are completely selfless and live your life completely for others, it is still *you* driving that self-neglecting bus. It's a decision that *you* make on a conscious or subconscious level. Deeper though, you really do care for *you*. All fear is the subconscious, buried *yous* trying to protect *you* from harm. When we see that life truly is a journey, and that your life—from the people who are in it to the who that you are—is always changing, we see that we actually do have the option to change *ourselves* even if we have less control of the world outside of us. We can choose to meet ourselves face to face. We can realise that who we are is not set in stone. We can accept with compassion that there are things about ourselves that we don't like, but also know that we have the ability to change those things. We can choose not to punish ourselves for the things we already feel deeply remorseful for doing. We can decide that the who that we are when we leave is going to be bigger, better, and more made up of love than the *who that we are* was when we arrived. Our spiritual journey in our human bodies is dependent on these bodies though, and sometimes we need a little help to get going. There is no shame in counselling, and indeed do read as much as possible from those souls further along on the road to becoming self-aware, which is the goal of all, whether we consciously choose to become lighter or darker souls. To know exactly who we are.

PEOPLE LIKE TO KNOW WHO'S IN CHARGE

Many years ago I found it somewhat creepy that the treatments of Eye Movement Desensitisation and Reprocessing (EMDR) and Emotional Freedom Technique (EFT) Tapping have proven so very effective in "resetting" faulty and harmful internal beliefs. It made me wonder for a moment if I was all just body after all and possibly imagining the whole immortal soul thing. This can scare you a little if you consider the fact that doing something purely physical can heal something mental or emotional when you have been taught for so long that the mind controls all. Then I learned that the body is not just a husk that we shed when we die, and that it must be just as much a recipient of our own love as our internal self. Our body is a part of our whole while we are here, and so not only should we honour it, we should learn more about it. Briefly putting aside our mental and spiritual components we should consider our corporeal self and how it forms the vital part of the woven tapestry that is our whole self that allows us to experience life in this physical plane.

Whether you believe that humanity only started out exactly as we are today at some fairly recent point in the past few thousand years, or that we are the ongoing evolving descendents of a billions of years old amoeba, you can't deny instinct. We all rely on, are helped by, and also harmed by our instincts and automatic responses to exterior input and events. Many base, course, violent, and other instinctive reactions are believed to originate in our "lizard" brain, and to be the result of actual chemical activities in our bodies designed to preserve our species, and particularly ourselves. I say that they are *believed* to originate there, because there are those who would say instead that these dark impulses or thought processes are result of our being fallen souls trying to live on a fallen world—the iniquitous results of the actions of Adam and Eve in the Garden of Eden—all of us apparently still trying to overcome their original sin. Scientific "proofs" having being so often disproved in the past few decades, there is nobody who can actually say that the real truth is any one of these things, or maybe a mixture of both—and maybe more. Some people believe that we are part of a game matrix. Little artificial intelligences living our lives according to the whims of some googly-eyed teenage alien gamer playing with his universal equivalent of The Sims®©.

Once again it's amazing how scientific evidence can seem to corroborate spiritual lore. The physical results (chemical bodily responses) to the actions and experiences of our forefathers are written into our DNA. Your ancestor having fallen off an unexpectedly appearing cliff into a gaping chasm while being chased by a hungry tiger might imbue you with a strange aversion to cat videos and an immobilising fear of heights. We find ourselves having unreasonable fears of things that have never harmed us personally, or we behave in certain destructive ways without seeming to have the self-control to stop. We instinctively like or dislike certain things. Through these fears and apparently helpless behaviours we can attract misfortune and unpleasantness in our lives. Some people would refer to these horrible things as the result of a biblical generational curse. Others would call it karma. Or blind bad luck in an accidentally created universe. Maybe the hand of God, or the devil and his gnarly minions. In a way some of these things can indeed be construed as generational curses—only delivered by DNA, and regardless of their points of origin they make up parts of who we are now. Believe this—none of that matters when the incredible power that is you—that you are—decides to have no more of it. Luckily we have the option to overcome these things. Once we see the source of something that is currently part of who we are, we have the power to change it. We really do have the power to start driving our own bus, and collectively, to change our world.

Rage, jealousy, fear, and their sometimes results of dishonesty, unkindness, or violence can leave us feeling guilty, ashamed, and wondering why we are so very, very bad when it comes right down to it. We want to know *why* we are here, *why* we do the things that we do, and *why* there is so much conflict and evil all around us. Our negative and apparently uncontrollable reactions don't make for feel-good loving feelings towards ourselves. It's horrible to feel dislike or repugnance for ourselves, so it's tempting to decide that they are not our fault after all. It's not our fault that we are made the way we are made, and it's not fair to blame us and make us suffer for whatever it was that Adam and Eve got up to back in the mists of time—is it?

One thing that we can't deny, no matter how far we try to insert ourselves into visions of happy bunnies and unicorns, is that this world is not entirely beautiful, at least according to what we see as beautiful in our innermost beliefs. Death, for example, is not something most people view with affection and joy. That doesn't only apply to humans. Animals don't happily embrace death either. Everything that is alive on Earth is mostly quite keen to stay that way. Some deaths are horrendous in our views. There is death all around us, constantly, in some form or another. Things are being eaten, accidentally squished, or wasting away in the painful ways common with some forms of disease all the time. Mostly, we, and the animals too, tend to focus on living as happily as we can. To see, taste, and enjoy the abundant beauty and life that there is in this incarnation that we all find ourselves in right now. Every now and then though, the darkness and pain that most definitely lives here along with us, rears its head in some unavoidable way. Those are the times, as unbelievable as it may seem at the time, that we can choose to make ourselves and the world around us just a little less dark, by not running away or giving in to negative emotion, but rather by *looking* and *assimilating*. We'll get to that later, although it is nice to point out here that by actually taking a piece of the darkness and weaving it into the light, then ultimately there is less evil "out there" because of that act. These small acts of looking and assimilating are vitally important to us as individuals, but even more so they are essential for the good of all. We have the power to do things if we choose to. Great things.

There's a widespread belief that everyone has a higher self. A self who is perfect, already in place at our core, and who we only have to discover. And that all the other imperfect stuff within is not really you. It could be true that our actual selves are one hundred percent pure, and I am not about to argue with those who truly believe that they have indeed connected to that divine centre of themselves. While I'm open to this being a fact—certainly that we have a higher self that we do need to become one with, I strongly feel that ignoring the other, sometimes not even close to perfect stuff that makes up *who you are* right here and now is done at your peril. I've read a lot of books telling me that all I have to do is look inside and I will see at my core a sinless, magnificent being. So far I personally haven't managed to do that. For me the question always arises that if we are perfect to begin with, then why sully our perfection with all the things that we do and deal with in our human lives? Why would we want to forget our perfection and experience what we experience? Why would we need to learn the hard lessons that we do if we were already all that we needed to be? I prefer to think of our original core as innocent rather than perfect, but that we become what we become in the *soul essence* of who we are as a result of the way we live our lives, and I'm sure that we don't suddenly become all-knowing and perfect again when our souls are released from our bodies. We have to at least nod in the direction of logic—even spiritual logic. If you insist on seeing yourself as distinctly different entities—ego separate from soul—then you cannot be whole. *You are you—the good and the bad. Please* don't try and kill your ego, no matter what anyone says. It is part of you. Teach it, grow it, but don't ever try to ignore or repress it or it will rise up out of nowhere one day and bite you or another quite painfully. Our souls may be immortal, but I cannot believe that they are exempt from being changed by our cognisant actions for good or for bad.

So having said that you must forgive yourself and love yourself, I know exactly how very very difficult that can be to do. Loving yourself is not something you can easily do when you've lived your life to this point not even liking yourself very much. Sometimes with victims of abuse they have a lifetime of conditioning to not love themselves, and when they've been abused by narcissists in particular, loving themselves can seem like joining with the enemy. Pretty much every single one of us has done at least one thing that we're deeply ashamed of. Forgiving ourselves can be much harder than forgiving others when we don't have the right thought processes. It seems much easier to not think about what we have done while lashing out at anyone else that we see doing something similar. We sometimes seem to have no control over our lives or ourselves. We definitely do not seem to be in the driver's seat.

When we look inside honestly we see a whole mixture of what makes us who we truly are, and quite a lot of it is certainly not going to be magnificent. The wonderful thing about that realisation is actually that it's alright to be imperfect. So to summarise—when we believe that we should be seeing perfection, we repress those things within us that we view as bad or wrong. By doing this we create a very much alive doppelganger within, which our refusal to accept or even see does not make go away. Jung called this the Shadow, and this desperate shade can have quite a lot control of our lives when we choose to not recognise it. We have to learn to plumb the depths of our shadows to bring all those repressed parts into the light before we can begin to work on treading the path to being whole, and it is in treading that path that we finally do begin to see glimpses of magnificence, because we don't only bury those things about ourselves that we view as bad, but also sometimes pieces of us that are beautiful, talented, clever, and *fabulous*, buried because others have taught us that they are not.

Our heads are full of thoughts from the minute we wake to the minute we go to sleep, and sleep itself is populated by dreams. It's a very busy place inside our heads, and we can wonder whether all of the voices in there are really us. Could it be the devil bringing the suggestion that we pocket the extra fifty bucks erroneously given to us as change? Is it God telling us to give our own fifty bucks to a homeless person? Is it our self, and do merely having these thoughts make us either good or bad in the end? Who is in there, and how do we know what the right or wrong thing to do is anyway? Just as we don't know what waits for us on the other side of our last breath on Earth, we won't ever truly know without having a good look.

Are you driving? If you are not sure then you should most definitely begin to have that good look.

PEOPLE LIKE TO LEARN

Whether people have been collectively, purposefully, brainwashed and propelled to the state we find ourselves in today, or whether it has simply been a perfect storm of the bad choices of leaders and societies, we must now fight to regain control of our selves, and to help each other do the same. In this world right now, from birth, everything that surrounds us, happens to us, and educates us, ensures that we have little or no time for self-reflection—in fact on our current course most people have developed a strong aversion to it. We immerse ourselves in the lives of others—often others we are not even slightly acquainted with. We make it our purpose to live for others. We make ourselves feel responsible for others to the point where those others become the actual reason for our own lives.

Most people are far too busy striving, worrying, and feeling both guilt and learned dislike for themselves to actually have any knowledge of themselves. They know their children or their spouses better than they know themselves, to the degree where if they suddenly developed a physical carbon copy of themselves that, apart from their physical appearance, they would have to get to know that self from scratch. While family and social interaction are important, it is much, much, more important to live your life primarily for yourself. This is not selfish. It is essential. But because of the way we have been conditioned it has become much harder to do than it should be.

Think about this for a few minutes. Everything that happens to us from the point of conception to our final breath has an impact on who we become. While still in the womb we are affected by our mother's feelings, diet, and habits. After birth we spend a brief few years at home (not including the abandoned or orphaned) before being sent to school, where we learn about a handful of things until we are old enough to work. The truth is that there is more than enough on this planet for there to be no need at all for poverty and starvation, but our education systems teach us otherwise. Our education encourages us to plan to do *real* work. It nips most creative dreams in the bud. When the majority, who can't afford university, leave school they do what they are expected to do. While there is no shame in doing the billions of low income jobs around the world that keep our current societies going, it is a very great shame that most of the people doing them are not doing them because they want to.

Most of the wealth of the world is owned by very few, with the rest of the population completely unaware of the fact that this is in any way wrong. The wealthy and the powerful who rule this world at this time are not going to willingly give up any of *their* wealth and possessions. They would rather make more. In order to do that, they need the working classes to continue to work—to have to purchase fuel to get to work, food to eat, education for children—to have to continue to maintain their allotted position in the system. The system keeps everyone far too busy to have time for much reflection. In addition to that people have very easy access to some of the worst drugs and things to eat and drink that are nothing short of poison. Our bodies are filled with toxins and our brains are occupied with things that are irrelevant to any sort of spiritual growth or awareness. We have no connection to nature any more. We can't see the stars in the night sky any more, and the very few pristine beautiful places left in the world are not often visited by the working classes. The only way that all of this could be even slightly acceptable would be if there truly was no purpose to our lives here. If this is all there is and there is no meaning to our existence then living our lives like this, filled with meaningless distraction, worry, pain, and mindless acceptance of the status quo might not be such a sin. But, if our lives should have purpose, and if this isn't all there is, then it is a sin against every soul on this world of such magnitude that it beggars belief. So what are you going to do about it?

It becomes obvious with focus. With the desire to help ourselves, humanity, the world, and all of the world's creatures. We begin with helping ourselves and the rest will follow. When we *look* and *see*, and learn and research, we realise that this is most certainly not all that there is. We have purpose, and we are here to learn, to grow, to become better, to become self-aware. While this world can seem like a scary thing to focus on with intention, and focusing on our inner worlds can feel the same, it is wonderful how liberating it is to face scary things. They tend to shrink in size and power when we realise our own power. We can do that. That is our purpose, in fact, to realise our own power, and the fact that we really do get to choose which path we travel, and to help our fellow travellers by doing so. We can create the path we choose. We do not have to blindly tread the paths that are laid before us after all.

PEOPLE RUN AWAY FROM THE BOOGEYMAN

There are those who insist that there will be no consequences for our actions as human beings. All is love and all is forgiven at the end of it all. While I can see logically how this should be true after actually *genuinely repenting* evil deeds, there are some people who are not at all sorry for the evil that they do. They wallow in their badness, and even though most of us cannot understand how anyone can actually enjoy winning regardless of lives crushed in the process, there are people do in fact enjoy this. There are very real sects that kill innocents as sacrifices to the ultimate evil. Human trafficking is one of the biggest "industries" in the world today. People—babies—children—all sold for various evil purposes. I really find it hard to imagine the perpetrators of these things dying and then skipping blithely through the white tunnel and getting a big hug from all those wonderful beings of light on the other side. I equally can't imagine them sloughing off all their evil thoughts and intentions to reveal a pure and magnificent soul self hidden beneath. They have become what they have become, and so they will remain until they choose to change.

Repentance is not simply saying that you are sorry. It is a horrible feeling—I know this because I have felt it. It is an overwhelming desire to undo something that you have done or caused to be done in the full knowledge that what has been done will always have been done, and there is absolutely *nothing* that you can do to change it. If you recognise that something you have done was truly bad and you are fine with it anyway, then I do not see how your action can be forgivable, but if you do, and if the doing of it makes you feel pain, then I do not see how it can *not* be forgivable. You must recognise that you constantly choose whether *who you are* moves into darkness or light, and I believe that these choices are the most important parts of your life. We often learn what is good and what is bad by unintentionally doing bad, but once we have learned it is always a conscious choice to repeat the deed. The choices that we make define who we become. We definitely do not leave this world the same way we arrive. We change every second of every day, and unless death truly is the end of it all, which is not at all logical, we will be either better or worse than we were at the start. Clearly there is a point to life, and with the fact that *we know the difference between the good and the evil that we choose*, it makes perfect sense that there will be some kind of result at the end of it.

I'm not talking about B movie scary monsters here. I want to call things what they are. By evil here I'm talking about the negative things in life—negative impulses and deeds mostly, and the reality of the source of them. Any impulse that could lead to the harming in any way of yourself or others is obviously not coming from a good place, so let's be aware of that. From the impulse to smoke or overeat, which hurts ourselves, to the impulse to murder, which hurts others, let us make ourselves *look* at these things. We need to know what we're up against if we are ever going to succeed in life. Let's begin by crushing that very negative trait of avoidance. We all love a superhero—how about digging out the superhero that already resides within each one of us, waiting to fight for one side or the other—just waiting for us to let it know which side we want to win?

Is evil real? Yes. It exists—it can and does have form. Because it has been created. The fact that you are reading this book probably means that you are considering the meaning of your life in one way or another. We wonder why horrible things happen to us and others. It's natural for humans to seek reasons for things. We think that it would be wonderful if everyone just treated others kindly—if murderers, rapists, abusers, and oppressors didn't exist. We strive to be the best we can be, and yet still, we have appalling things happening to us—we lose those we love, finances, stability, sometimes our minds. We wonder why. Some of us decide that there can be no God in such a system. Others decide that we must have been some kind of evil murderer in some past life and are now paying our karmic dues, or that we're reaping what we have sown in this life. No matter which way you look at it, it's very hard to justify the abuse and murder of a baby, or any innocent creature. Why punish an innocent, and if they are being punished for something that they really did do back in some other incarnation, wouldn't it make sense for them to at least know what it is that they are being punished for? Not one of us can answer any of these questions with absolute certainty. We can only do the best that we can with what we do know.

Most people are understandably not keen on pondering the existence of evil, and rightly so. It is dangerous to those who play lightly with it. The very word is scary, and almost all of us reason that if it really does exist in a very real way we want to stay as far away from it as we possibly can. The problem with this is that we *can't* get away from it. It pops up in the life of every single person of this world many times every single day in small and sometimes large ways. By pretending it doesn't exist we refuse to see it for what it is, and thereby it can do much more damage than if we were aware of its agenda. The truth is that when you shine light on darkness it dissipates—just so when you look at evil for what it is you realise that it's not as impossible to fight as you thought it was when it was only something in your imagination. It's a great shame that we give it so much power in horror movies, because the truth is that its power is *only* the power that we give it.

Have you ever found yourself in the presence of true evil, or looking at its residue in the actions or works of others? Of course you have. We all have. It is a real and powerful force in our world. Good is also very much a visible and sometimes tangible force, and one we much prefer to look at. No decent human being is going to want to immerse themselves in looking at evil. In fact a lot of spiritual practitioners recommend not watching the news at all so as not to let it sully your pure self. They say that good people shouldn't be looking at evil. For years though, I forced myself to do just that. I had some very good looks indeed. It's not fun, and it doesn't get easier with practice, so I understand. I have some horrible images in my head that I will never be able to forget. Regardless of that I don't regret looking, because I know now that avoiding evil, ignoring it, or simply running away from it allows it to grow in the shadows. Fearing it allows it to grow even bigger.

The most terrifying discovery of evil is when we see it within ourselves. Even the tiniest potential of it when seen in your own mind will have most people running for the hills, burying that bad thought or emotion and never allowing it to surface again. Or at least trying to. It is a hard fact to swallow that every human has the complete potential within to become anything, or to do anything, or to allow anything to be done, either for good or for evil. Our circumstances and our genes can give strength in making these potentialities within us more or less possible, but sometimes, confusingly, people will choose one or the other regardless of their circumstances or genes. The much loved child of perfectly "normal" heritage will take to enjoying inflicting pain, or the much abused child of a long line of violent degenerates will become a loving and kind teacher. When evil urges rise in children they will experience them in their innocence as rage, acting out, selfishness, hurting others, or any of the other many negative experiences we humans are prone to. Children process these things—it is how they learn—and choose their actions from there, *mostly*. Some children are treated horrendously enough to make personal choice nigh on impossible, but mostly children choose who they will become.

It is not easy to see when we choose evil because we tend to justify our actions based on the actions or lack of action of others. Even though rage is something that seems to blossom without our choosing it, what we do with it is always a choice after the first time we let loose and let it take control. We throw something, scream at someone, or hurt someone or something. Hopefully this occurs in childhood, and we are guided by gentle caregivers to see that we don't have to allow our anger to take the driver's seat. We learn that we can choose to remain in control and act according to who we want to be. Physically, rage is a whole rush of hormones, and some people can come to enjoy these heightened feelings. They can get a kick out of hurting others in their "justifiable" anger, even though on some level *they are perfectly aware* that hurting others is never justifiable. Is this choosing evil? Yes. It is.

So I'll say again, the *only* way to begin to overcome evil in any form, is to *look* at it and to understand that avoiding looking at it will not make it go away. Running away from it will not stop it. You have to face it down and choose its opposite. Obviously if you are in a physical situation where you are about to be killed by some evil person, they may indeed overcome you physically even though you are going to do your level best not to let them get it right, but that's not what I mean here. In that case run just as fast as you can. There are very many other ways in this game of life where our fear of looking at bad things or belief of our apparent powerlessness hands the win to the evil team. This avoidance of looking at evil is allowing a whole lot of evil to be committed in the world today, when the mere awareness of it by more and more people choosing to look will begin to challenge it, and eventually our choices as societies will hinder its proliferation.

Evil exists in small things that come in to your life every day. Tripping and falling on your face can be seen as malignant when you realise that there really is something out there in the ether that is quite happy to see you go down. When you wallow in pain and self-pity because you have been abused, that same something in the ether is even happier than when it was successful in causing those who hurt you to hurt you. Because now you are hurting yourself without any help from it. That knowledge alone should make you angry enough to choose to not allow any more of those dark victories in your life.

When you choose to stop living in fear, to forgive those who have harmed you, and accept exactly who you are, even if you feel that you are what you are as a result of their bad choices—when you take the bad things and use them to grow and possibly help others, then those evil forces scuttle away to look for easier targets, and you open up the space around you to be filled with good forces. Forces that will feed you impulses for good—courageous, creative, loving, and joyful impulses. Those evil impulses will never totally leave you, because your bad choices and internalised pain is what makes them feel what they think of as good. The difference for you now will be that you will recognise them when they come. You will be able to look at them and choose not to allow them permission to affect your life, your actions, and your thoughts.

I've always wondered why some people commit atrocities. Are they born evil? Are they not actually evil, but merely genetically challenged? Did they receive a serious blow to the head at some point? If you research the early lives of serial killers you will find that some of them indeed did seem to have things happen to them that could in some way explain why they became what they did. Head injuries, horrific child abuse, family history of violence. Others had apparently happy, completely normal childhoods, and came across as well adjusted, even wonderful, human beings to those who knew them. Why they enjoyed setting kittens on fire when they were toddlers remains a mystery. Nobody showed them how to do that, and they were labelled as not psychotic—fully in control of themselves and their actions.

Studies have shown that babies actually do feel empathy long before they are taught to be kind. Definitely if you are brought up in a loveless environment, where you are hurt, left to go hungry, and where your basic needs are deemed as unimportant to your caregivers, you are not only going to think very little of yourself, but there is a very real possibility that you will grow up to treat your own children the same way. Especially if you believe that as extensions of yourself they don't deserve what other children get either. Even the most sadly hurt children get to see what "normal" loving families live like. Friend's parents often become your secret surrogates, with you wishing that that mother was your mother. At some point we all realise that what was done to us was not right, and if we are very lucky, we do learn what unconditional love really feels like, both the giving and the receiving of it. Even though sometimes it can be hard to know how to give it if you've never received it, no matter how much you want to.

Love is not automatic, and the idea that it should be is one that can cause a lot of guilt and shame. True love cannot happily exist where fear is. That kind of "love" is another form of Stockholm Syndrome. Society has very fixed ideas on who we should love for no particular reason other than that we share blood. On the other side of the coin, love truly doesn't have to be earned. We sometimes love some very dodgy people. We give them our love and they give us something else entirely. I want to mention them in this section because quite a lot of what they do can only be labelled as evil. Enter the sociopaths and the narcissists. They seem to be increasing in number at an alarming rate, and just as the huge and tragic rise in depression and anxiety related issues, this is a very frightening reflection of our current societies.

Narcissism being officially recognised as an actual personality disorder is a relatively new thing, and there has been a huge explosion of the stories of the casualties of these critters all over the world. Thousands of websites are devoted solely to their victims while others are set up by self-confessed malignant narcissists who have reached superstar status in the eyes of the victims of others like them, and are making quite a lot of money simply by sharing what they feel and do. Even though narcissistic disorder and abuse is such a hot topic right now, it really isn't all that new. I think that there have always been some of them scattered around here and there. Only now there are too many of them to miss. In his book of some years ago one of my favourite authors, M. Scott Peck, called them The People of the Lie in his book of the same name. In that book he also pondered the possibility of them actually being evil, and suggested that that (being evil) be added to the list of psychiatric disorders.

I have extensive personal experience of malignant narcissism, having been on the receiving end from more than one. Are they evil? Possessed by demons? I still don't know. I vacillate between believing that they are one of those two things and feeling sorry for them because they will never understand what real love is. We might say that they love themselves, but I believe that what they actually feel for themselves at the core of their beings is loathing and terror. Pride on the other hand they can and do feel. Their self-complimentary ways are due to pride, not love. If they really could feel love, or if they allowed themselves to go through the pain of looking within at themselves, they might be capable of change. Or maybe not. Logically, there can be no real love in a malignant narcissist. Even though they sometimes come across as very loving, it is only in order to get something to stoke the fires of their constantly ravenous pride. The extreme "love" they show to a pet dog for instance is not love—it is pride that the dog loves them unconditionally, and the attention that they give it is purely to secure more fuel in the form of doggy or other adoration. Animal "loving" narcissists can be very confusing when victims are trying to figure out who or *what* they are dealing with.

Are narcissists evil? I do believe that they become so. When we know what is right and what is wrong, and this seems to be something born in most of us, and we *choose* to do what is wrong, then that is evil. You are the sum of your parts. Your parts are everything about you. What makes you *you* are your thoughts, beliefs, likes, dislikes, loves, hates, and your *actions*. If most of what you think is that you are better than others, thoughts of envy, hatred, revenge, wanting to harm, then yes, you are mostly evil, because that is what *you* are made of. It doesn't matter if there is a tiny speck of good in the middle of all of that bad unless you dive down and battle through the murk to fetch it and make it grow. And grow it will if you try by the way, no matter how much murk you have inside—the power of good—is the greatest power there is, but you have to invite it into your life. Either way we invite what gets to live within us.

Good won't force its help on you. You have freedom of choice—you must understand how important that is to your existence, and to what you inevitably will become. It is humanity's freedom of choice that has got us into this terrible pickle and it will be our freedom of choice that will either save us or sink us completely. Are you aware of how different you are now to who you were ten years ago? Even though you hold the pieces of every self you have ever been, you are a completely different person to the one you were back then. Even your physical self is completely different. You become what you allow to change you. You grow. You could grow stronger from challenging life experiences or you can allow them to crush you. You choose. Imagine how wonderful this world would be if more humans chose good over evil more than the other way around.

Humans know the difference between good and evil—big good and small good—big evil and small evil. This seems to be where mankind sinks or swims, no matter how we came about this knowledge. We have free will *and* this knowledge now. People who honestly believe that whatever they do doesn't matter in the great scheme of things have my deepest sympathy, because whether or not these things matter in the afterlife, they matter greatly to who you become. I believe that at many points in every life we get to choose good versus evil, and I do believe that there are consequences. If you only ever make choices that are evil, in other words choices made from selfishness, greed, hatred, rage, vindictiveness, malice, how could you not become evil? Eventually that small spark within you that holds the potential to be good is snuffed out, and evil you will be forevermore.

Denying the reality of good and evil makes life a lot more difficult to live. Knowing that your enemy is real is the first step to defeating it. Even when simply accepting it being done by others and not ourselves in particular produces ripples. Ignoring evil is just as dangerous as accepting it with open arms. We are seeing more and more of the results of people ignoring it and denying it all the time.

Why do people do bad things? Why do people do good things? The answers to these questions are surprisingly simple, and the reasons for them are also at the root of all that ails humanity and this world today. Fear causes a whole lot of terrible things to be done by basically good people. Love causes people to do wonderful things. Fear is the most powerful tool in the evil toolbox. Apart from the few individuals who are truly evil, and they do exist, most of us don't plan on being abusive or purposely hurting anyone or anything.

Anyone who believes that the world humanity has brought about today is good, or even civilised, is seriously misled. As a species we are getting things entirely wrong, and as individuals we are becoming increasingly unhappy. More and more people are experiencing severe depression and anxiety. Anyone who has had a full-blown panic attack or experienced the lonely, self-despising apathy of depression will appreciate how debilitating these things are.

It is interesting to note that mental illness is not something commonly seen in wild animals, but is extremely prevalent in those kept in zoos, factory farming situations, circuses, and in creatures experimented on for "scientific" purposes. Humanity's current behaviour is causing this rise in mental and spiritual ailments in ourselves as well as in the other inhabitants of Earth. These mental aberrations are almost always the result of being abused in some way. We no longer recognise certain practices as abusive or evil for various reasons. This does not make them any less evil, and it will not stop their eventual impact on ourselves and our species.

Abuse doesn't have to be a beating. Abuse can also be being deprived of any of most of Maslow's hierarchy of needs, which are real requirements for mental wellbeing. This pyramid of needs consists of five tiers, the bottom three most basic tiers consist of food, water, warmth, rest, safety, security, intimate relationships, and friends. These basic needs are not automatically given to the population of this planet at this point in time. Many children spend their early lives in terror rather than feeling safe or secure. Many adults find themselves without anywhere to rest peacefully. When these things are not in place, or worse, when their opposites occur, mental stress is going to be present. There will be fear and anxiety in abundance, and from there come all the problems of that are growing bigger everywhere we look in the world today.

Is it possible that those who govern our societies are unaware that simply being born to the "wrong" family today equals poverty, hunger, and fear is a bad thing? An evil thing? An unnecessary thing?

PEOPLE DON'T WANT TO BE THE BOOGEYMAN

People have gotten away with murder because it was proved in a court of law that they had no control of their actions. Legally that is. But doing something terrible because your emotions got the better of you at the time doesn't change the fact that you have done something terrible. Is the act of taking a life less evil because the one who did it could not control his or her rage? That is not a question that has a definitive answer and there are very many guilt-wracked people in the world who have had their own lives ruined because their feelings drove their actions without them having time to consider what they were doing. They may have avoided time in jail, but they will never escape the knowledge and the memory of what they have done. If possible it is always better to have the ability to consider what we do with our emotions.

Not everyone has a problem with acting or talking before thinking. Rage issues often are the results of past abuse, but can most definitely be worked on even so. Some people are more stoic than others. In fact, practising stoicism has been a real thing for quite a while. These days when we call someone stoic we tend to think of it simply as being a type of self-control or indifference, but what it really meant to the philosophers who created the practise of it back in the third century BC, according to the Concise Oxford Dictionary was *making virtue the highest good, concentrating attention on ethics, and inculcating control of the passions.* People have tried to be better at being people for a very long time. A little bit of stoicism would do our failing modern world a whole lot of good, and certainly, it is important to at least be able to control ourselves. To have our own opinions on what is good and what is evil, and to act accordingly.

Love, affection, joy, fear, anger, hatred, cravings, self-pity, empathy, calm, unhappy, inspired, sad, guilty, insulted, proud, bored. We experience one or another emotion for all of our waking lives, and this is quite natural. Some feel good, some feel bad, and sometimes we don't feel much in particular either way. Many feelings are instinctive, and the only thing that separates us from animals in this respect is the fact that we know the difference between right and wrong, so our reactions to these feelings should come from a place of choice rather than simply acting out on the spur of the moment. The truth is that we do have a say in how we react most times, as long as we learn to look and think before any action arises from sudden emotion.

The world we are born into is not one we have much control of. We have no say over where or when we are born, and no say over who our caregivers are and how they treat us when we are little. There are rules and laws in place that we don't get to dispute. We have to go to school. We have to have money to live in houses the way others in our society do. We have governments who decide whether or not we will war with another nation, and when it's alright to kill or not to kill. We don't get to roam around and hunt to feed ourselves. There are systems in place. We work. We buy food and other necessities from shops. We are taught that we must eat three meals a day, and that these meals should include all the currently accepted major food groups. It's much easier to go with the flow, so we mostly choose to do that. Still, even if they are sometimes hard, there are always choices to be made. Self-control or lack of it helps us make choices, and again, simply, you choose whether or not to exercise it. What you exercise grows stronger.

Losing control of yourself is a terrifying thing. You have to ask the question, if you are not in control then who, or what, is? If *you* are not in control then *what* is in possession of you? Where do thoughts and impulses come from? How about those dark thoughts that pop into your mind that make you wonder about the goodness of your own innate makeup? Do they come from within or without?

Self-control is a little easier when the thing you know you are likely to impulsively reach for, if it is a physical thing, is not close at hand. This will give you time to examine the impulse and try to consciously make a decision whether or not you will act on it. When an impulse arises in the form of anger, such as the impulse to lash out verbally or physically in response to a perceived or actual slight or attack you have to very firmly and quickly get to *focusing* on your urge, what it is and where it is coming from, before acting out on it. This is very difficult when you have spent your lifetime giving in to urges as they arise.

When anger strikes there are more than two choices. We think that either we let rip and give in to the feeling, striking out verbally or physically without even trying to control ourselves, or we completely stuff the feeling, without allowing ourselves to feel it for more than a second or two. There is a third choice. Not an easy one, but the only one that is going to cure you of ever losing control of your anger again. You must let it come, but you must look at it inside only. Sit on your hands and bite your tongue, but feel every bit of that rage. Close your eyes. Ask yourself where it is coming from, and why it really arose. Often the cause of it has nothing to do with what is currently taking place. We must learn to examine our emotions before allowing them free rein.

When I was younger I had a terrifying temper. I would let rip without at all considering any outcomes, and some very horrible outcomes there have been because of that. It isn't easy in the beginning to stop in your tracks when in the grip of a powerful emotion, but it most certainly can be done, and the more you do it the easier it becomes. Whenever you are filled with a powerful emotion *literally* stop in your tracks and be still. Look inside and take the time to have a proper inspection. Consider why it is there. Consider what you could do with it. You will find that the more you look at your emotions the more you find the most surprising reasons for feeling them, and once you have the reasons you can prevent future tragic outcomes. Often simply knowing why they are happening will stop them from happening again.

Learn to be as stoic as possible while at the same time being as loving and kind to yourself as you can. People do a whole lot better in life when they knowingly take responsibility for their actions. As societies and as people we must begin to stop blaming anyone or anything for our own deeds, even if our deeds sometimes arise from the seeds of hurt planted by those who acted horribly to us. It is all about the choices we make whether or not to allow anything or anyone other than ourselves to *make* us do anything at all.

PEOPLE LIKE TO KEEP PEOPLE

Grief is part of life. Physical death is not required for grief to come calling. It comes in different sizes. From the smaller mourning of a loss of a job, a friend, a beloved old vehicle, small betrayals, to the all encompassing, body and soul filling agony that follows the loss of a great love. We grieve for many things. People mourn the loss of childhood to abuse, or sometimes even the lost opportunities for closure or restitution. They sometimes grieve or even feel guilt when their abuser dies. They mourn the loss of a whole lifetime when a child dies. They mourn the loss of a pet—those beings who truly know how to love unconditionally in their innocent perfection.

Humans have a great capacity for this kind of pain, and even though we try very hard to avoid it, we seldom can. Instead we must learn to live through these hurts. Unless we *choose* to hang on to pain, we will be stronger when it finally fades to a throb, as all pain naturally does when we allow it to. If you manage to suppress grief somehow in the belief that if you squash it for long enough it will disappear, you will hurt yourself much more than living through it. You will find that grief is patient. It will wait without at all diminishing if you ignore it. Everything that happens during the course of our lives—every thing— every thought—every joy—every pain—all of these things remain within us always. All of these things have lessons in them that we can accept as great gifts, and it is only when we embrace them and walk with them they finally fade and shrink—they dissipate and leave us stronger and wiser.

Someone told me once, when I was in the throes of great grieving, that grief never really goes away, and that terrified me, because for me there has never been a greater pain than that. Day after day I would wake up with that awful ache that remained with me until I fell asleep. I fell asleep afraid of the pain I knew I would feel the next morning when I woke up. I bought piles and piles of books on the subject. I spent hours online looking for the magic pill that would ease my hurting heart. Some things were helpful and others were not. It was good to find out what the stages of grief were, because when you have stages you generally have a beginning, a middle, and an end. The truth is that for the rest of your life the grief will pop up when you least expect it—a photograph—a smell—a little yellow feather—and it will gut punch you and be just as sore as it was when new—thankfully though of a much briefer duration.

The first problem with grief related to the death of a person or any creature that you love is not knowing for sure that they are alright wherever they are now. Are they alright on the other side of the veil of death? Suddenly you question your formerly staunch belief in life after death and wonder if they really did die only for the very essence of them to be extinguished forever. You think about the not so fabulous things that they did—their sins—and you wonder if they could possibly be burning in hell, or enduring an eternal frigid aloneness apart from God. You miss them. You even miss the things that irritated you about them. You miss their aliveness.

This might sound a little strange—or not if you have ever experienced the love of an animal, but the grief that I felt when one of my two little Weaver Birds died was hugely more painful and terrifying than when humans who I cared for passed away. The problem with pets or animals who come into our lives one way or another, and who we fall head over heels in love with, are deemed by the world as "just animals". Not in possession of souls or destined for Heaven or Hell as humanity apparently is. Worse still are those beliefs that animals get absorbed into some sort of species collective unconsciousness after they die, and lose whatever individuality that they had while alive forever. I couldn't bear to think of my most beloved Button the Weaver Bird being stirred into some sort of Weaver Bird spiritual soup, to return over and over again as another Weaver Bird made from scratch who would never remember me and his bird family who so clearly mourned his passing too. With humans we "know" that they retain who they are wherever they go when they die. So I once again read piles of books and articles on animal afterlife, and came across some very scammy money making sites claiming to communicate with them, and also a couple that seemed very credible. Finally I accepted what I had *known* all along, with a little help from a whole lot of impossible only yellow butterflies doing impossible things around and on me many, many, many times in the middle of winter. I also pored over accounts of near death experience trips to the afterlife for mentions of animals, and I can tell those of you wondering where your beloved pup, or cat, or goldfish is now, there are most definitely all of these beautiful creatures, with their very own personalities intact who will be very happy to see you when you also move on to the next stage.

Grieving isn't only about the death of a human who we have loved, or sometimes haven't actually loved, but become accustomed to having around for a very long time. We grieve when we are told that we have an illness—we grieve the loss of youth. There are many opportunities to grieve in life. It is true that some people don't grieve much. Some people don't seem to have the capacity for great grieving, but unless they know something most don't about life, death, and the eternal truths, and live joyfully because of that, these people are not to be envied. I would much rather love enough to feel the pain of loss or separation than not.

According to Elisabeth Kübler-Ross and David Kessler in their book *On Grief and Grieving* (which I highly recommend if you are having a problem with prolonged mourning), the five stages of grief are denial, anger, bargaining, depression, and acceptance. These don't necessarily happen in this particular order, and each one of them will last for as long as it lasts. It's helpful to understand what you are experiencing, but at the end of it all, only one of the above will help the pain dissipate and that one not as much as time. Acceptance will help, but you have to go through the time too. It also helps if you believe in an afterlife. In all honesty the more you love and are loved, the more you may grieve when you lose that love in this life, and that particular kind of pain and sadness can be oddly beautiful in its intensity.

Every one of us is completely unique. We have different baggage. Every experience in life colours who we are—who we will become. No two people have the same reactions to anything. We have different levels of empathy. We have different strengths and weaknesses. Sometimes we will cling to our grief and our day to day lives become coloured with anxious thoughts and sadness. When our grief is mixed with guilt we can do ourselves great harm. Again, some of us have much greater capacity for holding on to guilt. It is important to remember that grieving is actually a healing process in itself. Accept these painful feelings as they come. Try and immerse yourself in them for a while. Not too long a while, because as important as it is to recognise your loss, it is just as important for you to continue to live. There is never, ever, any merit in wasting the life that you have in a never ending immersion in pain. And when the big grieving is over, your life will once again be filled with other things and other thoughts, except for occasionally when a memory will slice your heart just a little. At times like that hold the pain and honour the love that brought it, but only for a very short while. You will meet again when the time comes. For now—live.

PEOPLE CRACK NUTS

Why am I afraid to dance, I who love music and rhythm and grace and song and laughter? Why am I afraid to live, I who love life and the beauty of flesh and the living colours of the earth and sky and sea?

The Great God Brown - *Eugene O'Neill*

Rather than be labelled as crazy or weak, many people will hide depression, unusual habits or addictions, and any number of other things not accepted as normal. These are usually the symptoms of some kind of hurt and do not in any way make anyone less than anyone else. If you whack your eye on a doorknob it is going to hurt. Emotional whacks will leave you with pain and scars too. It is normal and you're not crazy because of it. Not everyone is badly abused, and some people are not completely aware that they have been abused even so. Most people are certainly unaware of how badly they abuse themselves. When people have been badly abused there are always results. Even those who have never been so damaged can benefit from knowing these things, because it is very unlikely in this very broken world that anyone can travel through life without coming across at least one battered soul, in one way or another. You might simply have been abused by too much stress, or poverty and loss. There are many things that can abuse you. You will have results, and again I say, that does not mean that you're gaga—you just need a little self-awareness. When you know you, you can set about getting help for you if you can't help yourself.

Mental illness has been stigmatized for hundreds of years. People who were thought to be mentally defective were locked away where they could not hurt anyone while in the throes of whatever kind of madness they appeared to have. Terrible tortures have been carried out in the pursuit of healing some of these people. Perhaps people are no longer being shackled to walls or being lobotomized, but there certainly is still huge stigma, and many modern treatments are more damaging than the supposed mental illness they are intended to heal. Giving medications that numb out perfectly logical symptoms of spiritual or emotional injury is like putting a band aid on an infected gut wound—that thing is going to fester underneath there. Clearing out the dirt and sewing up the cut will be more painful at the time, but at least it will heal.

Admitting to having a mental breakdown can effectively lose you friends, respect, jobs and opportunities. People keep what they believe to be abnormal secret. Depression, anxiety, addictions, habits, and anything that makes you appear different in a bad way are not things people like to talk about. Sometimes the consequence of being afraid to share these taboo illnesses is the loss of life, by never getting to live life as fully as possible either by becoming frozen and locked away inside yourself, or by the actual physical ending of a life—suicide. Hopefully this will change and people suffering in these ways can be helped, because other than actual physical or chemical mental ailments most of these things can be healed with understanding.

Once you hit the point of breakdown—cracking—meltdown—anything you want to call it, you are in trouble indeed, because nobody reaches such a point without severe trauma. Either one huge traumatic event, or a whole lot of ongoing trauma that is not necessarily visible to anyone. It is truly amazing how good people are at concealing their own pain. The good thing about breaking down is that hiding is no longer an option. You are not going to get up again without taking action. But know that if you do take action, your life can become better than you ever could have imagined. Certainly much better than it was on the path towards your final collapse.

Breakdowns happen because of overload. Something will have been wrong for a long time, and eventually, usually after avoiding addressing what was wrong, you reach a point of no return. You can't take any more stress or fear. You can't run any more—you can't hide—and so you stop. A breakdown is your mind, body, and soul telling you that you have to look *now* at what is wrong in or around you, or else you're not going anywhere. You've just hit bottom. Here is where you get to choose. Either you stay broken or you address what broke you, and you get up again, no matter how slowly and painfully, you get up and become a whole lot better than you were.

Depression, anxiety, addictions, and other related "mental ailments" are not abnormal. They *are perfectly natural reactions to "abnormal" events and situations.* Modern life is not at all *normal* insofar as what we as living sentient beings require to remain *normal* ourselves. So what is normal? When you are getting up every morning and spending the best part of every day for the majority of every year of your life doing something you absolutely hate, it is totally normal for that to depress you. You don't admit that this is happening because everyone else does the same things. They work because they have to live somewhere. They have to eat, and not freeze to death in winter. They have no choice. Logically this is true. After all, if everyone on the planet suddenly decided to stop working because they hated it, what would happen? So you carry on, trying to ignore the depression as it gets deeper and stays longer.

Anxiety is normal if you are regularly abused, verbally, spiritually, financially, or mentally. These things are like when you cough and sneeze when you get the flu. They are simply normal, if unpleasant, symptoms of your body, mind, and soul trying to get rid of something that does not belong in there, something that is doing harm. Having a panic attack is your body telling you that something is wrong. Being regularly and deeply depressed is your body telling you that something is wrong. Addiction is your body telling you that something is wrong. Not something wrong *with you*, but something wrong *for you*. The fact that you don't like your job, and feeling bad at your lack of gratitude for even having a job when so many are starving and jobless, does not mean that you are abnormal or bad. The fact that you are sad because your soul knows what true freedom is and that it is not what society is selling doesn't mean that you're loopy. The problems arise when you pretend that you are grateful, and keep your hatred of your job and your life to yourself, and carry on spending your life doing what you don't want to do, while despising yourself for hating it. Double whammy right there. You hate the way you are living your life and hate yourself for hating it. Not being depressed and anxious in such a situation would be abnormal. I'm not suggesting that you quit your job and head off into the sunset with no money and no plan. You must first honestly assess your situation in this world as it now is. I am suggesting that you look around you with honesty and logic, and totally absorb your actual reality. Once you can truly see *what is*, you can begin to work on fixing your situation to cure what ails you. Slow and steady as you need, in the knowledge that how you live is as important as what you become by the end of this life, and that these choices should be your own.

Even though change terrifies most people, change is not bad. Humanity these days is stuck in a situation where you are born into a world with seemingly very few choices. You can't simply head out into the wilderness, mark out a camp for yourself and live there, hunting and foraging when you need to and contemplating the meaning of it all when you're not admiring the beauty of your world or socialising with your neighbouring campers. A very few people own and control most of the world's resources, and the majority of other people own very little. People are dying of starvation while other people are throwing tons of food away without batting an eyelid. Animals are being tortured in their thousands for food. You must accept these things as normal, because if you don't you will be labelled weird—a crazy tree hugger. The fact is that these things are both wrong and unnecessary. There are better ways for us to live. Kinder and less damaging ways. They are only happening so that a few can stay very wealthy. You know this, but you are not allowed to know this if you want to fit in, so you try and convince yourself. Unfortunately you can't "un-know" what you really know at your core, but admitting to this knowledge could get you excluded from the herd. Humans are wired as social animals, and being kicked out of our herd is perceived as a death sentence. So you shut up and go with the flow, pretending that all is just as it should be. Sooner or later that is going to make you feel bad. Bad enough to hurt you quite badly.

Not everyone breaks down, and not everyone has chronic anxiety or depression. Most people can cope with short bouts of stress, which is in fact good for us, but in this modern world where stress is much more constant than it should be, more cracks are appearing in more people. Lifestyles that would have been considered torture a few decades ago are now the norm. People have no time to do much other than run, run, run. We have lost touch with ourselves and the real Earth, and the only way to begin to get out of our messes, whether they were brought on by abuse or merely unwise lifestyles, is to find ourselves. That is the first step. To look. We must stop being ashamed of our own feelings, and we must stop being afraid of being put into the mental disorder box because of perfectly natural symptoms. Healing ourselves and our world must be our new priorities, no matter what anyone else thinks or says about us, if we are to live meaningful lives without too much regret at the finish line.

Sometimes I think that life would be a whole lot easier to live if we categorised things into two sections—good and bad according to our own beliefs. Try to do one and avoid the other. Simple. Unfortunately things have become a whole lot more complicated. Mental illnesses and personality disorders are categorised on lists. Some are considered harder to treat than others, and some are considered quite manageable. Others not so much. At the core of most treatments is the patient's desire to get "better". Narcissists, for instance, do not want to change because they know that change will mean a painful process for themselves, besides they mostly are quite happy as they are. As their modus operandi results in the pain of others, which they generally enjoy, they *choose* to remain as they are. In fact, recovering from any personality disorder is never a comfortable process, but people do it. Many of those with Borderline Personality Disorder (considered by many to be incurable) work through incredible pain and fear, but they do it because they do not want to cause pain to others or themselves.

The field of mental health changes all the time as studies are done on the mind and emotions, as well as the body. Some problems are caused by damage to the brain, or differences in the brain that are there at birth. Tests done on certain serial killers have revealed huge physical aberrations, showing the physical brain of the true psychopath, and bringing into question whether or not they are responsible for their actions at all. It is a hot topic. One researcher into this particular subject found that he himself had the physical brain of a psychopath, yet he had never experienced the urge to kill or hurt anyone or anything. It has been deduced that other factors must come into play. Some serial killers have nothing physically wrong with their brains but still their empathy for others is switched off, and they get their jollies from causing and seeing pain in others—they are the sociopaths. While the hurt they are capable of, and do inflict is the same, it appears that the psychopath is born and the sociopath is created, either by being themselves abused—or by something else entirely—something evil.

If the current mainstream belief that consciousness arises in the brain is true then diagnoses should always be easy, as in X happened so Y will follow, but that is not the case. While genetics do play a part, apart from the proven genuinely purely physical cases of mental aberration, there is always one wild card—the consciousness of the person involved, and whether or not they choose one path or another. Few choose paths of extreme pain, but some do, and they overcome these "illnesses" while others choose to either stay the way that they are, or find solutions to their own pain down the dark road of hurting others. I am personally aware of taking the painful road because it has been my own, and I can confirm that it is not only doable, but at the end—wonderful. Regardless of the path you take, you never go back to where you were before you were so wounded that it caused your mind and emotions to slip into "mental illness". The probability exists though, that you will be so much stronger that when the pain or fear does try and get a grip again in the future you will find the immense strength needed to fix it straight away. Just like any muscle grows with worthwhile exercise, which itself is hard and painful work, your emotional and spiritual muscle grows and becomes incredibly powerful as you take yourself through the mire of what is hurting you.

Recovering from serious trauma damage incurred over a lifetime is not an overnight process, and it will never be truly fixed with any sort of pill, but with this understanding it can be managed to where you can enjoy a *natural* and fulfilled life. Many natural processes are considered abnormal, when in fact they are not at all. Pain is a natural part of sentient life—any life. It is natural to grieve—people do it and animals do it. It is natural to be sad sometimes. *It is natural to react to cruelty and torment.* The caged bird that runs up and down madly or self-harms by pulling all his own feathers out is suffering a perfectly reasonable reaction to being imprisoned and controlled. Wild creatures do not behave this way, but we have inflicted many of our "madnesses" on "domesticated" animals. This shows us how normal it is to become depressed for no apparent reason—or anxious—or angry. There are always reasons, whether apparent or not.

Once we are aware of this, we can get to work on accepting what *is* and making it better, even though we can never cut it out. It is by turning our weakness into strength that we heal. We assimilate our damage rather than running from it. We recognise it as a part of who we are—a part that requires our own love and patience. We enfold it rather than cursing it, and this loving enfolding moves us along the path to wholeness and awareness of self.

Trauma is not only brought on by obvious and accepted forms of abuse. Humans aren't designed to live the lives we live today. There is an overload of everything, and everything is getting faster, louder, and more painful. People have lost control of the personal journeys through their lives. They have few choices. The feeling of having to get up and go to work every day when it is the last thing that you want to do is in itself torture—not laziness. Top that feeling with the feeling that there is something wrong with you for feeling it, and having to force yourself to simply get through the days of your life that you hate, and you have an excellent recipe for a "disorder". Having to be constantly connected and available online is only natural to a computer—humans are social creatures, but not to that extent. We breathe poison, we eat poison, and we have moved so far from what our bodies and minds desperately need that we have become *collectively disordered* as well as individually disordered. When we see that fact, we realise that "mental illness" is a symptom of the state of mankind at this point in its journey rather than something that should hold social stigma for any individual. It is our current reality, and all of those who can see this should begin to try and fix it with a sense of extreme urgency, because it really is all for one and one for all at this point. No matter how "normal" and fulfilled you feel that you are, we will all sink with the already badly listing ship that is humanity today.

PEOPLE FORGIVE

While forgiveness truly is most helpful to ourselves, it is a bad practice to try and force victims of any sort of abuse to forgive too soon. Forgiving can seem impossible, but forgive we must, and strangely, it is only when we finally are able to truly accept forgiveness from ourselves for our own real or perceived faults and actions, are we able to truly, instantly, forgive literally anything in anyone else. It is not so much an action, but rather a deeply peaceful feeling. So we do not need to be rushing out and raining blessings down on murderers or shouting from the rooftops that their actions are all good. It is merely accepting that we cannot understand their motivations, impulses, or indeed how far they have allowed themselves to be influenced by the evil that is so real in this world working tirelessly to cause humans to embrace the darkness, fear, and rage that it offers. It is hard to choose good while in these human bodies filled with hormones and chemicals, and the ego, all trying to pull us in different directions at the same time no matter what our true self wants to do.

Humans can work at changing ourselves and our world without hatred, recrimination and violence. These things only breed more of the same, and so we are left with a never ending circle of growing evil as good people choose to attack rather than defend and attempt to change the evil that they do see from a place of love. From a place of love, we see how hard it is for ourselves to do this being human thing, and as we forgive ourselves for our own weakness and sometimes terrible deeds, it becomes natural to forgive others for anything. There is no switch, and getting to this point is not always easy, but it really is something to strive for continually, because forgiveness is the only first step we can take to healing our world and ourselves.

If humanity is going to survive forgiveness must become a priority. It should be obvious to all that without it we're heading towards disaster as anger, guilt, and fear drive our actions, both individually and collectively. We must understand that forgiveness is not weakness. It is not condoning. It is not saying that it is alright to continue to behave in hurtful or evil ways. It is not saying that anger, fear, and guilt are always inappropriate, but rather that while these things are both right and helpful feelings, holding on to them and using them as reasons to react in more hurtful or evil ways are disastrous for all of us. Angry nations go to war. Toxically guilty people cause pain to more than themselves when they decide, consciously or unconsciously, to punish themselves for the balance of their lives on this planet for whatever they did "wrong".

There is a lot of information out there, both in spiritual teachings and also in physics, suggesting that reality is a kind of tapestry, stretching out infinitely in all directions, and that time as we see it does not exist. There are merely points in the tapestry, and everything exists at the same "time". It is terrifying to think that dark acts committed, on purpose or not, will forever reverberate in the spot that they occurred in. How could we ever fix such terrible things? Moving forward and doing better is the solution. The new perfect pieces of the tapestry will weave into the dark pieces, making the whole of it better.

The objective here then would be not only to forgive yourself or others, but to be genuinely remorseful for your action, or to genuinely feel forgiveness for those who hurt you, and then to move on. You don't have to forget, but you do have to not mull over the hurt. You can mourn your loss or the loss you caused, but you have to move on. I believe that if you do not truly forgive then you hurt yourself or keep the hurt you caused another alive forever. If those who hurt you feel no remorse because they are basically evil, you can still weave light around their deeds in your part of the tapestry until they no longer have power over you.

Don't believe that those who hurt you will have a happy outcome, even if they appear not to be bothered, or even pleased, by the hurt that they caused you. Remember that they live in hatred, self-pity, jealousy, unhealthy self-adoration, and fear, yes *fear* is at the bottom of all of those other feelings, because all of those feelings begin with fear. Just as you choose how to react to fear, so do they, and they choose to hurt others to cover their own pain. Understanding that revenge is not the answer is important, and neither is hatred and unforgiveness, because those things will rot your soul away. Know that we all pay for our choices one way or another, in this life or the next, and they will pay for what they did to you as surely as the sun rises every day, without you having to waste any of your life on them anymore. Pity them, for they have ended up in a very dangerous hole, and concentrate on your own joy in creating a new life of love for yourself and others. Always choose love over fear, and hatred, self-pity, and jealousy will pass you by.

The key is always *intention* and *remorse*, but the biggest deal is love. If you can truly love yourself and others you will see that we are all stumbling, trying to find our way, including ourselves who we judge most harshly. You will find when you look that mostly, except in certain cases, evil intent is not all or even most of what you see. Focus on the good and kind, the sweet and caring attributes that you can find, and love your way to forgiveness. Love is more powerful than any force in the universe, because it is the greatest power in the universe, and when you truly use it you will always conquer without striking a blow, or giving or receiving any pain.

Remember that there is hurting and death all around. It is natural even though it is not natural to enjoy that part of life here. Still we must accept it, and sometimes we must forgive it. It is not possible for any creature to live on Earth and not kill, intentionally or not. In the ten commandments the law is "Thou shalt not kill", not "Thou shall not kill other people but everything else is fair game". Nobody and nothing was designed to live on Earth forever. To live without killing or causing something to be killed is impossible, so how do we get it right? Again we come to intent. It's good to remember that we arrive here alone, and we leave alone. It stands to reason that if there is an accounting to be done it will be for ourselves only. It's understandable that when we are hurt we get angry, and if that hurt causes us great and lengthy pain we hold a grudge against the perpetrator. If the person who caused you damage feels remorse that's wonderful—mainly for them even though it might make you feel a little better that they know, admit, and are sorry. The truth is that most of the hurts we inflict on others are not intentional, and when they are those few who will actually hurt on purpose do so for their own gratification and feel nothing at all about your suffering. Sometimes the knowledge of your pain will give them actual pleasure. So your hanging on to rage and the results of what they did to you will hurt *only* you, and it will hurt you for as long as you choose to keep it constantly alive in your awareness as a part of your current reality. So for our own peace and growth we must forgive those who have caused us harm.

This doesn't mean that we have to invite those perpetrators into our lives whether they are sorry or not. We don't even have to tell them that we have forgiven them. Forgiving isn't condoning or accepting what was done as alright. It is choosing to acknowledge that what they did was evil, and yet still not to hold anger, hatred, or any other form of spiritual unease within you because of what happened. You move on purposefully and choose not to allow those who hurt you to continue to hurt you. Accept that they will get whatever is due to them without your further pain.

True forgiveness has not got anything to do with words. Saying "I forgive you" might help the person who hurt you, but it will not do a thing for you. Saying that you forgive someone to yourself won't mean much either if you don't really mean it—even if you think that you do. Forgiving is more vital to your own wellbeing than anything else. Having unforgiveness in your heart will prevent you from being able to heal whatever hurt has been done to you, and also the effects that that hurt has had on your personality, your life, and your faith in yourself. True forgiveness removes the pain of victimhood and grows strength and empathy. Keep in mind that the abuse that you suffered is not a licence for you to be unkind, uncaring, or abusive to others. Never try to get recompense from those who certainly do not owe it.

Every self-help resource worth its salt, from bestselling soup for the soul books to the bible, tells us that we must forgive others for ourselves and also forgive ourselves. It is true that living with unforgiveness poisons our souls and can taint every moment of our lives. Living your life as a victim means living a life of loss, so forgiving is important work to do if you want to live the best life that you can. What does it mean to live your life as a victim? It's kind of like a badge of honour with some people—myself included in my younger years, and it can only hurt you further, in that victims have a tendency to attract more abuse, and waste their lives constantly wishing for things to have been different in a past that cannot be changed. This way they continue to harm themselves long after the fact, going so far as to dislike themselves for having been abused. This is not necessary. Regret should never be the biggest part of anyone's existence, and self-abuse should never be at all.

One thing that you must realise is that what you expect from others, you also expect from yourself—even if subconsciously. If you can't forgive others, then that expectation of perfection will apply to you too. When you make mistakes during the course of your life your inner self knows that you find this unforgivable—not only in others— just simply unforgivable, and so you will never get over your own bad deeds, which are inevitable in every human life. We must learn to understand and empathise, hard as that is. Most people don't get up every day and plan to hurt others. They have their own fears and problems to deal with. Don't confuse your inner/subconscious auditor. I'm going to repeat that in the hope that you will really absorb it. *If you can't forgive, then that inner part of you gets that— you can't forgive—the end. You can't forgive someone else, and so therefore you can't forgive yourself.*

Sometimes we take something, or many things, all awful things, that someone has done to us, and that is all we can think about them— their terrible deeds become who they are for us. While understandable, this is very unfortunate, because it's really unlikely that there are many humans who are totally one hundred percent bad, and if they eventually do get to that point, they will probably have much more intense agendas than abusing one or a couple of small defenceless people. I have been guilty of this at times, refusing to see anything likeable, funny, *loveable*, kind, beautiful, or any other fabulous thing in those who have seriously damaged me. It's a horrible place to be when that happens, because you can't seem to move on in any facet of your internal striving to heal. When you do force yourself to accept that what your abusers did was not necessarily who they were, and you take the time to empathise—even if only for a little while—for whatever it was that happened in their lives that caused them to hurt you as they did it will help you greatly. Try and see them as humans, just as you are, with weaknesses and strengths, and failings, and be grateful that you have managed to come to this point where you are strong enough to examine both your own and their possible hurts that cause hurts.

PEOPLE WEAR HAIR SHIRTS

Most of us are good at guilt. Some of us are too good at it. We're guilty because we have much and others are starving. We're guilty because we hurt someone's feelings, whether on purpose or not. We feel guilty when we eat chocolate or drink wine—we even call these things guilty pleasures. We're guilty because someone implied that we should be. We feel it when we aren't working hard or when we choose to watch a rerun of a favourite series for an entire day when we know that there's a sink full of dishes and only leftovers for the family lunch. Writers and other creatives feel it when they're doing what they do best because the whole world has made them well aware of the apparent fact that doing what you love is not considered proper employment. So what should we do? Carry on as usual and just live with the guilt? Stop doing all of the things that make us feel it? That one will bring on some powerful self-pity, I can assure you. Or is it possible that maybe we should accept that there is absolutely no reason to feel guilty when doing or having something pleasant, with the proviso that having it or doing it doesn't actually harm yourself or another. How do we get rid of all the guilt?

If you have much, give some of it away—that will stop guilt at the starting gates. If someone is hurt because you choose not to do what they want you to do, that can't be helped. If you do what you don't want to do then you will be the injured party, and it's unlikely that the person who is trying to get you to do something that you really don't want to do will feel any pain at all. There's nothing wrong with enjoying life's pleasures—we are here to experience life, and life experience includes pleasure. Life can be good if you allow it to be most of the time. If you eat too much or drink too much and to the detriment of your health and wellbeing, know that you *don't have to*.

It's up to you, and so whichever way you choose with this there is no point in guilt. You choose your own path. We were not born to suffer—we were born to live, love, laugh, learn, enjoy. Yes, pain is inevitable, and so we learn and grow. Pain is a powerful teacher, but there is no need to hold on to it when its season passes. We were not designed to wallow in pain or guilt and self-hatred.

Then there are the darker reasons for our remorse and shame—the valid ones, and those are the ones that can lead to completely wasted lives. Lives wasted unnecessarily. It is not easy to contemplate the fact that *you* did something cruel, hurtful, or hateful, regardless of whatever "reason" incited it. It's much easier to try and completely forget the act, or to blame it on someone or something else. We can blame it on someone else by saying that we only did it because that particular someone abused us and instilled in us a lack of control because of the abuse, or we can blame it on something else by saying that we can't help having a temper because we're Irish, or Italian, or whatever other group of people feel that they are entitled to be hot-tempered by virtue of their genes.

We prefer to believe that some other thing was in charge when we committed the nasty thing that we did, because in actual fact, we are really kind, loving, and generally nice people. There is no way that an actual part of us could or would knowingly ever do such a terrible thing. Until we accept that it was indeed ourselves who did the deed, regardless of the reason, we can never truly forgive ourselves because we're holding on the belief that we didn't do it in our conscious mind, while our subconscious is fully aware of the fact that we did do. This conflict is confusing at the best of times, and dangerous at the worst—both to ourselves and to others. If we truly believe that we are not in control of what we do then we are quite capable of doing such things again. We must accept our imperfection, and love ourselves regardless of it—because of it. We must strive to do better, but we must know that wearing a hair shirt for the rest of our lives will not change anything. While we can't turn back time and prevent whatever it was that has caused a toxic guilt to taint our lives, we can most certainly change the future.

Accepting that we have done or said something that has seriously harmed another is not an easy thing to do. Mostly we prefer not to think about the things that make us feel guilty or like bad people. Luckily we know that feeling like that is good, because it makes us realise that truly bad people don't care when they injure. We could also believe that trying to make amends would entail admitting to something that nobody apart from ourselves actually knows, or even bringing something into the present that has been buried for years or decades even, and thereby taking a chance on losing who and what we love and care for now by making them see that we aren't as nice as they think that we are. Know this. *It is not necessary to announce your mistakes from the rooftops*

If you've made mistakes as a parent, and deeply wounded your child without realising that that's what the outcome of your past actions might be, then you might want to try and help heal your child's wounding (if it is still affecting them) by admitting your mistake to them, asking for their forgiveness, and helping them understand how deeply you regret your actions. If you've harmed another—human or animal—you can go out of your way to help other humans and animals. One thing is for sure—you are not the only person ever to have done what you did. You can help prevent others from making the same mistake, or you can help those that have been on the receiving end of similar mistakes. Leave the guilt behind and replace those emotions with love. Love can turn your terrible deed into a blessing in a way, because if you had not done it you would not now know enough to try and prevent it from happening to others.

I have seen very small children commit horrible acts of violence towards other children and animals. Most of these children have had homes filled with violence, abuse against them, poverty, and lack of love and guidance. That's not to say that perfectly well treated and loved children never hurt each other or their pets, but generally only mentally and spiritually injured people do these things seemingly on purpose. Adults who emerge from terrifying and tumultuous childhoods often go on to raise their own families in similar circumstances. They somehow manage to cut off their own empathy and live their lives in angry victimhood, raging at an unfair world and uncaringly destroying innocents. Others go the opposite route. They become self-aware. They understand—they forgive—they do good—they strive to become better and to live their future loves with love, empathy, and to draw a line and move on from whatever was done to them and also whatever they did. No matter how bad what was done to them or what they themselves did was. Without this line, a happy future is almost impossible. You must choose whether you go to the dark side or the light.

Some people have no problem forgiving themselves. This is not always a good thing. When we can justify even horrible things that we do, or find some way to blame them on others, then we lose out on very important life lessons. Self-forgiveness cannot truly be of any benefit when it is based on the justification of an act which harmed another especially, and blaming others for our own actions is basically choosing to not face or accept what we have done wrong when we were aware, on any level, that what we were doing was wrong. At the other extreme of this, when we do accept that we have done something terrible, and then accept the lesson in the action by having remorse and repentance, we can also then commit another terrible act by refusing to forgive ourselves regardless of these things—we can go on to consciously or sub-consciously punish ourselves for the rest of our lives, by sabotaging any possible good that could come into our lives. Deep down in our shadow there is a *knowing* that what we did was "unforgiveable", and so we make sure that we never allow happiness, financial success, or joy into our lives. We might not realise that we are doing this, and often blame these things on our childhood or various other abuses inflicted on ourselves. Even so, we must forgive.

The thing is that it is quite common for victims of abuse to inflict abuse on other beings as they act out their inner torment. Unless they are psychopaths or people without empathy, they are at some point going to realise that their actions have inflicted hurt on another, even if that realisation only arrives years after the action. Such as when an adult ruminates on their childhood "sins". They feel huge remorse, and then are torn between the facts that what they did was indeed evil as they now realise, and that not only would they never do anything like that now, in their adult state, but that they would find it difficult to forgive another person for doing what they did. What a very difficult situation to overcome, and the more empathetic, loving, and caring the sufferer of this self-hatred has become at this point in time, the more difficult it can be to forgive their past action. Punishment becomes the order of the day even though you are no longer that person at all, so in effect you are punishing yourself now for the actions of a you who is no longer in residence.

Self-forgiveness can be something that is almost impossible to give to yourself when you realise that the one you hurt does not forgive you. Apologising and asking for forgiveness might help, but what if the one you hurt is not contactable, either because you really don't know where they are, or because they are dead. Guilt can arise from hurting an animal who is long departed. Even when this was because of lack of education or a temporary loss of control—especially as a child who was not treated as well as they should have been—this can cause huge remorse and guilt. Difficult as it is to accept when you've been beating yourself for years or decades, is the fact that your remorse and new knowledge, and also the fact that you know that you could never do such a thing again, should be the end of your self-punishment, and the beginning of your self-forgiveness.

When you have large guilt you likely will live a lie. Either you will hold on to the belief that you are a monster and make sure that everyone around you understands that, or you will cover your sins with a whole lot of syrup and be as sweet as can be in ways that are not at all true to yourself. You don't want whatever you feel guilty about to be seen by anyone else, so you run, hide and lie—you can't risk anyone (often including *yourself*) seeing you for who you think that you "really are" because of it. The truth is that who you really are is *not* that one single thing that you did, and all the running and hiding only ensures that you never get to meet your actually wonderful true self—and neither does anyone else. If you feel guilty about doing something, then you might have imposed a subconscious sentence on yourself. We can self-impose sentences of not being allowed to ever enjoy any part of life without even realising that we have done. We must head inside ourselves and find out more in order to release ourselves from this kind of unnecessary bondage. Many of the things that we feel guilty about were also committed by an unconscious part of ourselves.

When you won't or can't forgive yourself you add to the limiting beliefs in your life, which are already holding you back. As well as the regret, shame, and at the far end of the spectrum—self-hatred, you take hold of beliefs related to things that you have "done wrong" about *who you are*. These beliefs either allow or disallow success in your life. Make no mistake, what you believe can literally hold the power of life or death for you. You can indeed develop a mortal illness purely from your belief. We don't realise even a tiny little bit how powerful our beliefs are, or our faith. Faith isn't only a religious thing. If you have utter faith in the fact that you will die from cancer because both of your parents did, you very likely will do exactly that.

When I say believe, I mean *really* believe. People wonder why nothing changes in their lives when they zoom around for days on end muttering positive affirmations—putting into words their desires and wants for their lives. You can do that for years to no effect if you don't truly believe that you deserve these things. If you have unforgiveness inside you towards yourself, you are not going to allow yourself to succeed no matter how many affirmations you rattle off each day. Often, even if you think that you have forgiven yourself for something and moved on, there is a part of you inside that is saying, "Uh uh. You deserve to suffer for what you did, and I'm going to make sure that you do.", without you ever being conscious of it. Until you address this particular part of you head on, and get it to accept your self-forgiveness and your total acceptance of happiness, success, and growth for *yourself*, you aren't going to go very far.

Some of us are much harder on ourselves that we would ever dream of being on others. We can actually be incredibly abusive with ourselves. Certain people will claim and hold on to every "bad" thing they've ever done, and beat themselves up for their whole lives, while never ever owning the good things that they probably do more—or the truth of the nice people who *they* really are. Sometimes what they view as *bad* is not actually so. Accidents don't happen because you are bad, they happen because accidents happen. That's the way of this world. Sometimes when we combine our victim mentality with our guilt it becomes even harder to move on from, because what we did becomes inevitable following on from what was done to us, so not only do we accept our innate badness, we expect to do more of it. We can believe in our own badness even while blaming it on someone else—another double whammy right there. We accept our badness believing that we have no power to be anything other than what we have become.

We can become so wrapped up in mourning our own imperfection that we lose sight of the fact that if we were already perfect there would be no point in being here. Imperfection *is normal*. Making mistakes is normal, even if those mistakes have horrible consequences, either for ourselves or others. We're all in school here, and in order to learn we must not allow ourselves to crumble in the face of our own perceived faults and past wrongdoings. We must learn from these things and become better by doing so. We can become so much better precisely because of what we have done, because we can understand the things that led to our actions—we can understand enough to help others who are still on their knees and wondering how they will ever find the strength to stand up again. By understanding, we can forgive, and once we have forgiven we really can move on to brand new things knowing that we will never commit the same mistake again, and why, while our compassion for others and ourselves grows exponentially, as it should. It's alright to mess up—royally sometimes—and it's alright to accept that you are a good person—talented, kind, fabulous, beautiful, deserving of love and success, in spite of the messes, because they are indeed part of life.

The sad thing is that truly bad people, who could do with a bit of self correction don't care about harming others or being selfish, lazy, or unkind. People who generally are good and strive to do their best and not to hurt anyone can punish themselves severely for their slip-ups or perceived sins. We need to learn to accept that we are going to get quite a lot of things wrong, and there will be times when we will inflict harm on others with or without intending to. When we realise what we've done, and deeply regret it, we can choose to fix the situation if that is possible, learn from it, and move on, or we can believe that we ourselves are inherently bad because of our misdeed and mete out some kind of self-inflicted revenge.

I have spent most of my life trying to punish myself. Yes, I've made wrong choices. Terrible choices. I'm human and I had a really, really bad start out of the gates, and for my first couple of decades. I have not ever made one of these horrible choices out of malice or from a place of not caring—rather from places of naiveté, lack of knowledge of wrong and right—especially lack of knowledge of the rights of safety, unconditional love, and from being shown from birth that fear is the way to control rather than the giving of love and leading by example.

We can also punish ourselves because of the perceptions of others of our actions even though we know that we never intended them harm through those actions. I made a lifetime "job" of blaming myself for everything, and also for taking on blame that was never mine. I do have blame for my sins, and I accept that, but no longer will I accept blame for no reason other than that someone else has assigned it to me if they refuse to accept that it was never my intention to hurt them. You can regret outcomes, but it is not honest or reasonable in such cases to wallow in guilt and self-recrimination.

It's easy to say that what is done is done, so move on and forgive yourself when you have actually done something very bad. When you have really inflicted serious emotional, physical, or spiritual harm, or even caused the death of another. If you've ever hit an animal with your vehicle, obviously unintentionally, and felt really horrible about hurting or killing it, multiply that feeling by hundreds and you come close to understanding how someone would feel who harmed someone they actually knew and cared about through stupidity, lack of attention, or outright uncontrolled anger. Not everyone has done something so terrible during the course of their lives, but there are those who have, and unless they honestly did what they did on purpose and in full awareness of the evil of their actions, they need to be allowed to, and to allow themselves, to forgive themselves and move forward without wasting their own lives any further.

Just like forgiving others does not condone what was done, forgiving yourself does not condone or justify what you have done. You have to take the bad and try and use it as a base for good. Unless you really want to spent the rest of your life immersed in the pain of your terrible action, you must spend some time with it in yourself—in other words you're going to have to sit quietly and think about it— then you decide what (if anything) you can or want to do about it— then you move on to your life ahead without punishing yourself any more.

A lot of self-help books and articles suggest that you share what you did with a trusted other. I don't believe that shaming yourself to the world by telling all the gory details is the way to go, unless *you* are keen to do this to help others by showing them what not to do. Equally, think carefully before shaming another publicly no matter how badly they hurt you or others—once it's out there you can't take it back, and revenge is seldom as satisfying as the anticipation of it might have seemed. We tend to sort sins by the size of them, so if we feel that we have never done anything *that* bad we get to judge and talk about others, but the truth is we have all done bad things, so we should at least try to have a little empathy. Sharing with another human is not a requirement for forgiveness or for self-forgiveness, but sharing with yourself and with your God, or Creator, or whatever you call the One who loves you unconditionally, is. If you honestly don't believe in a God who actually does love you unconditionally and really does want to help you, then I ask you to consider it for a moment. For one moment open you mind and call out for help, and you might be surprised that help will indeed be forthcoming. You don't have to be religious to pray.

Never lie to yourself because you can't ever run away and hide from you. When I say you here, I mean the one who is mostly overlaid with emotions and rampant thoughts as you go through your days. The quiet you within who actually does know the difference between good and evil, but often has a hard time surfacing from the surrounding layers of pain and confusion that life will create over time. Admit that what you did was wrong. Admit it to yourself, and own the fact that *you* did it. Not the devil, and not the prior actions of anyone else.

That's hard and it hurts, but it is necessary for you to know that you did it.

The next step is to find out why you did it—not to justify it, but to understand it and to turn it into a foundation for good in your life. Was the start of the action an uncontrolled emotion? Was it fear? Was it rage? Was it purely accidental? Accidental is the easiest cause to face. Buried emotions such as fear and anger are going to be more difficult because you're going to have to find and heal their beginnings. Many people aren't aware that they have rage inside them because they have buried it so deeply in their shadows that it isn't something that anyone generally sees until at a time of great stress, fright, or shock, it appears, seemingly out of nowhere and literally "takes you over". If necessary do some work on your shadow self. I highly recommend Debbie Ford's book *The Secret of the Shadow* and *The Shadow Effect* by Deepak Chopra, Debbie Ford and Marianne Williamson, for help with how to do that. Finding the root of the impulse that caused you to act as you did once again does not justify what you did. The deed is still wrong, and you did do it, but you will now realise that the part of you that did it was an unconscious part—not the conscious *you*. Do the work needed to integrate that part so that you will be able to spot it immediately if it comes again, and immediately choose not to let yourself go and give it control. Awareness and knowledge are indeed power.

As I said, another great way to ease the pain of guilt is to make amends in some way. Again, this is not a requirement, but it will not only help you—it could be a very great help to others. If it's not possible to make amends directly to the one you harmed for whatever reason, then consider doing something good and selfless somewhere else. You could donate to various caring causes, or actually get in there and do something more tangible yourself to help those suffering or in need. If you've hurt an animal the same would apply—there is a lot of pain in the animal kingdom on this planet directly caused by humans—they can do with all the help they can get.

Finally, realise that you are not the thing that you did. Your evil action does not make *you* evil unless you enjoyed it and have no qualms about doing it again. Don't give it head and heart room every time it surfaces after you have done the above. Move on with your life having learned not to do it again, and even though twinges of regret do rise occasionally, accept them for what they are. Your genuine remorse. You can't change bad things you have done in the past, and you must not allow them to destroy your future. Make evil good by turning it to something useful either for your own improvement, the improvement of others, or both.

Self-abuse is not something to be proud of no matter what you've done wrong. It is in itself wrong, and if you waste your life by spending it in constant self-hatred and self-recrimination you don't in any way atone for anything, so if that's what you think you are doing—*stop it now*. You are human. *All* humans make mistakes. Some mistakes seem worse than others, but there can only ever be one take-away from them whether or not we can fix them, and that is to learn from them, and then to move on using that knowledge to try not to make them again.

Compassion and understanding strikes a killing blow to evil committed, thereby allowing the conduit through which it previously flowed to heal. Hatred, anger, and abuse are all facets of evil, even when directed at yourself—by doing this you're putting more points in its tally. Evil is as real in our world as the ground we stand on, and by allowing it further control by hating ourselves defeats the object of the growth and education of our soul. Just as we should have compassion for those others in its thrall we must have compassion for ourselves. By accepting its reality in our deed, we thereby see it and by seeing it we bring it into the light of consciousness. That is enough to ensure that now that we have looked at it squarely, the next time it arrives we will recognise it and not allow it free passage through us again. Yes, what you did was bad, but you didn't do it on purpose (consciously), and now that you know that you can consciously choose whether or not to do it again. If you do—then you knowingly commit evil, and you're unlikely to feel any guilt. Once you *know* it is though—you won't do it again. You've learned a lesson which will make you grow into a better human being—you can share what you've learned to help others if you choose, thereby helping others to become better human beings also—you learn compassion for others and for self—all works out for good—but it's important that you move on from there to whatever future lessons await you, because nothing at all is gained from a wasted life.

Shame can destroy lives just as surely as guilt can, and even though we may believe that it is all the same thing, it isn't. Shame is about who we are and guilt is about what we do. When we're ashamed of ourselves we don't like who we *are* as a whole, and it is pervasive no matter what we do. Guilt can be added to shame in ways that is simply proves how truly bad we really are. But we have to like ourselves—love ourselves warts and all if we are going to make any sort of success at life. There is no reason to ever be ashamed of being human, so we must dig down to the roots of it and get rid of it. Shame begins in childhood, and mostly from within our family units. There are no schools for parents, and we have to make do with the ones we are born into.

Shame is not a bad thing when it's appropriate. It's not a bad thing to be ashamed of something we have done wrong. Allowing it to stay too long and become a shame of ourselves entirely though is very unhealthy, and also unnecessary. Shame is meant to teach us, not to torment us. Very few people will openly talk about the things in their lives that they have done wrong, especially if these things were done because of selfishness, greed, or anger. We hide our dark deeds, fearful of others thinking badly of us because of them. It is true that we are judged by our actions. People decide "who we are" by what they see us do, and if they only ever see us doing one horrible thing, that action will form their opinion of us as an individual. You could be saintly your whole life and have a moment of loss of control due to any number of possible stressors, and act out physically before thinking, thereby hurting another. If you tell anyone what you did who doesn't know your usually saintly incarnation, they will see you as violent or abusive, and generally not someone they'd like to have in their social circle. So we keep these shameful things secret.

Our views on what is terrible are different. Many people think that physical punishment is just fine and dandy. In fact if you think about humans in general we are a physically violent species. We are all killers of something. Even the most gentle of souls wouldn't bat an eyelid at squashing a bug. We poison rats without feeling overly bad about the horrendous way that poison kills. We smack our dogs and sometimes our children. We consider the killing of enemies to our nations as righteous rather than murder. We might not actually still kill the animals we eat ourselves, but we are aware that they do have to be killed by someone in order for us to eat them, and most people are alright with that fact. Physical violence sometimes happens as an automatic response, and when we see ourselves as inherently good and that happens to us, we are suddenly faced with the possibility that we are not in fact good. Shame arises when we lash out and hurt someone or something that we love or respect in some way, and it is very particular to each one of us depending mostly on what we were taught as children. Two people could hit a puppy too hard for chewing their best shoes, hurting it more than intended, and one of them could walk away without a twinge of regret while the other would feel instant remorse that would stay with them for a very long time.

That shame is not actually telling us that *who we are* is bad, it is telling us that who we are doesn't want to *do* that bad thing. That shame is telling us that who we are is good, because if who we are really was bad then we wouldn't feel any shame. This is a good thing except when we make that hurtful action a part of who we *are*. Feeling shame of yourself as a human being entirely is very bad. We need to see and accept ourselves as we are, with all of the good and evil that we have done without hating ourselves either because of the way we've been treated or the things that we've done. So—if we feel guilt or shame about something that we've done then that in itself is good, but shame of who we are is bad. Life is all about choices for good and for evil. Sometimes these choices are hard. Sometimes situations dictate that choice is removed, and we do something from a place where we feel that we really don't have a choice, and when the outcome from that action is bad we feel shame/sadness even though we never did what we did in the knowledge that the outcome would be bad, nor from a place of malice. If something's true for you then it is your truth, and hating or abusing yourself for creating a bad situation without the intent to create a bad situation is absolutely pointless.

Shame can be instilled early in life by caregivers, teachers, and peers. When a child is made to feel of less value than others because of neglect, abandonment, physical or mental abuse, poverty, race, or many other things and combinations of things, they take these things on board and come to believe that it is true. They really are less than others, and so toxic shame of self sets in to stay. Overcoming this kind of shame is not easy after a lifetime of belief, but there are treatments that really can help. Talk therapy and inner self exploration can really fix such terrible brokenness. If you are constantly being horrible to yourself it is a very good idea for you to seek out help, and if you can't afford a therapist then try and find an online group—there are many out there ready to help. But even without this, shame colours our lives in unnecessary ways.

Shame can seem overwhelming. It can consume you and cause you to falter very badly. It's painful, and can seem like a pain that will never leave you. People show each other all the time that being a different colour or religion and many other perfectly normal things make you a lesser being. We must learn not to believe these things. We must learn that we are perfect just as we are, and when the small shames come when we stumble, we must learn to let them go. Once again working on your shadow will help if toxic shame has you in its grip, and the two books suggested earlier in this chapter will help you to work through it.

PEOPLE SAY THANKS FOR ALL THE....

During the course of all our lives things happen, or not, that we regret. We lose people we love, and sometimes we gain people who we come not to love but can't seem to get away from. Missed opportunities. Mistakes we made. Stupid choices we made, or stupid choices other people made that hurt us or those we love. Mostly regret will take the shape of a short wistful moment of "if only", but sometimes it can take over a life, leaving its victim in a state of perpetual sadness, believing that because of their loss or pain, that their life is ruined—finished—having no further or possible purpose. This is a terrible state to get into, and a very difficult one to get out of. It seems hard to see anything to be grateful for from this vantage point. Also from this vantage point, there is not much more irritating that some sunshiny Susan telling you to count your blessings. Still—

Genuine gratitude will bring you more blessings that you can believe because the power of thoughts and words is a very real power, and what you truly believe and ruminate on will bring you more of the same. We are branching in to Law of Attraction territory here, but that's alright, because it is a real law of this universe, and not at all in a witchy or weird way. The forces for good and evil that exist in our world will happily give us more of what we believe. If you believe that you are useless, poor, and a total failure, then you will be given that. If you believe that you are worthy of receiving joy and abundance, you will be given that also. The key words at the beginning of this paragraph are *genuine gratitude*. You can't pretend to be grateful on the inside no matter what you say externally. It is the energy of your true emotions and thoughts that will bring you what you get. If you want to practice gratitude and you feel blocked from truly feeling the feeling, then you once again need to dive within and inspect your shadow. There is a whole lot more to be grateful for on this world than we sometimes realise.

If you take the time to examine your life and look for the positives you will be amazed at how much you will find to be grateful for. The very fact that you are alive means that you can continue to learn and grow as a soul—which is your very purpose for being here. Being grateful for having endured pain, and learned from it is another reason for gratitude. Growth it generally painful, and from suffering you learn compassion for others and yourself. You learn what you believe. You learn what is wrong or right according to who you really are, and you learn how to react when these things show up in whatever form. I know that this is a very old chestnut, often rolled out at very inappropriate times, but the real truth is that no matter what you are going through right now, there is someone going through much worse, and that alone is indeed something to be grateful for.

Counting your blessings, no matter how few or puny they appear to you, with genuine, heartfelt gratitude will bring you much greater blessings. Don't count and dwell on your trials and tribulations, and don't chew over the injuries that have been dealt to you, no matter how awful they have been. You merely add to the injuries by continuing to suffer mentally and emotionally from the deed or deeds long after they are finished. It's a little like cutting your nose off to spite your face, it serves you no good, except to raise unhealthy chemicals in your body and mind, and in dwelling on evil you get its attention, and so it will deal you more evil.

Decide to begin to give more time to positive thoughts, and to inspect and evict negative thoughts as soon as possible. When anger comes, let it in, examine it, and if there is nothing good that you can do about the cause of it try as hard as you can to move on from it. Concentrate on what you *can* do to make things better for yourself. Forgive if you want to, and you should want to, because you can forgive purely for yourself. You don't have to tell those who harmed you that you have forgiven them, and nor do you have to invite them back into your life to possibly do you more harm. You don't have to have anyone in your life who you don't want there—even if they are wonderful in their own right and have never done a thing to harm you. *You* control who gets to spend time in your space unless you are a child or helpless in ways that make you physically unable to prevent it.

It is important to take control of all that you are when you are able to do so. Look carefully at your choices before deciding that you truly are stuck right where you are, because those of us who do choose to fight for our freedom will often someday have the opportunity to use what we have learned on our journeys to help those who truly are helpless—voiceless. Even though those who tread this path often seem soft and by extension, weak, the truth is that those who truly understand and embrace absolute love from without and within, and realise that there is no evil thing, deed, person, or entity that is powerful enough to win in the end—because it is the end that *really counts*—become truly powerful themselves. Sooner or later we must all decide which side we will choose, and when we do we often discover warriors within ourselves that we never knew existed, which when fuelled by the strength and power of love can move mountains, and truly make a difference in this sadly hurting world of lost and damaged souls. Gratitude is a powerful first step to personal growth.

Sometimes it seems as if blessings are a long time in coming even though you are grateful enough for your current state, but never question the timing of your outcome. Things generally happen right on time. You probably have another lesson to learn. Accept them all as they come—the faster you learn, the more you will grow into all the things that will make you happy—all the wonderful blessings that are waiting for you just as soon as you are truly ready to receive them. Along the way you may find that the blessings you thought you really wanted pale into insignificance beside the ones you have already received. Have patience and faith. You will find that there is always more than you think to be grateful for right now.

PEOPLE LIKE IT BIG

Extreme fear is sometimes instilled from childhood and is ongoing into adulthood. It's like the alien from the movie of the same name that springs up and attaches itself to the actor's faceplate and drills its tentacles—its roots—deep within his whole body, finally jumping out at will, destroying its host in the process. Fear can engulf when it is lifelong. It sends down tentacles that bury themselves in a physical manner throughout the system. When the victim finally reaches the point of strength—enough strength to try and remove them they come out slowly—reluctantly—and even when they do, they leave holes. Holes that leave you shaking and weak, but nevertheless, holes that can heal stronger than the surrounding tissue, just as broken bones heal stronger than the virgin bone around them. Fear can be overcome.

Bear with me for a few short paragraphs as I wander into the "unknown". One of my favourite things to do has always been to lie on my back and look at the stars. I stopped doing that years ago and forgot about it mostly until I started working on my shadow self. There it was, hiding away from the condescending remarks that had sent it there. It is back again, filling me with joy as I gaze up, imagining the life that is buzzing around those twinkling stars. I've always been fascinated by the universe and what it is made of. Over the years my research into the things that both interest or affect me has led to some startlingly simple facts. Even though these are logical, we humans are forgetful, and as this life tosses challenges, things that just a few days ago gave you peace slip your conscious mind. One of these facts is that even though fear is useful in small doses when it comes to running away from lions, in all other respects it is completely unnecessary.

Often when you overlap science with the esoteric, science overlaps neatly and pretty much proves the esoteric. People talk of the afterlife when science tells you that they were clinically dead for long enough for the brain not to be able to work. Science has preciously told us that consciousness lives and dies in the brain. New and exciting research is beginning to reveal that consciousness does not in fact arise in the brain any more than the man who operates a computer is created by it. The conundrum is that the person whose brain could not possibly have been able to function at certain points will insist that their consciousness had been eyeballing the death scene from the ceiling, going on to repeat what was said or done by onlookers or doctors, from *outside* of the body. The amount of reports such as these means that it would not be logical to accept that our consciousness does die with the body, regardless of where it begins. Our brains change according to our emotional responses to various things. Our consciousness grows regardless of our physical selves.

Parts of the brain light up in response to pleasure and other parts to pain. This happens during these events, not before them. Bessel van der Kolk showed in his book *The Body Keeps the Score* that our emotions physically change our body and our brain—which is why ongoing trauma is so dangerous. *Energy* puts us in motion and *energy* bounces between the synapses in our brains—our brains *can't create energy*. Physics teaches us with the Law of Conservation of Energy that energy can only be transformed—never destroyed. Therefore logic informs us that the energy that mobilises our bodies and brains has to go somewhere when our bodies no longer contain it. Physics also proves that only about four percent of our universe is visible to us, but that the rest of it is not simply empty space as we used to think. It is filled with what is called dark matter and dark energy. That 96 percent has mass and gravity that has physical effects on our visible universe, so logic again dictates that there is definitely something there, just not in any dimension visible to the human eye. That to me justifies most accounts of the afterlife—it is not as if there isn't enough space out there for any number of heavens and hells.

I'm always amazed at how hard people try and disprove any possible evidence that we are spiritual beings who will go on after this life when they so desperately want it to be true. Religions have certainly mistranslated and cast aside some of the ancient texts, but even with what we have to work with now it is clear that the ancients had no doubts about the fact that we continue on after physical death. If all these things are true and if you spend the years that I have spent researching what we currently know about different aspects of our reality and then trying to see if they all fit together somehow, you will find that common sense shows that we do continue, no matter what happens to us here and now, in forms more fabulous than we can imagine. So then, what is there really on this world to be so terrified of? I understand that the past few paragraphs may have caused a few eyes to glaze over, but I wanted to put it out there anyway. What is the worst that can happen to us on Earth, and will it have any effect other than to teach us something else as we head on into that mysterious 96 percent that we can't see yet? It is worth thinking about, no matter whether you believe in it or not. There is certainly no reasonable fact to think that this is all there is or will be, and the sooner we start working on our inner—energetic—self, the better. Our inner strength will grow and impact us from right now, no matter what happened to us before. This gives us a reason to not give up, or to give in, and to begin to claim our own power. Now—thank you for your patience with my side-trip—we can go on to the kind of human fear that we have no doubt at all is real in our current lives, scientifically or otherwise.

Fear can be graded. It can be so slight as to be almost unfelt, or it can be so huge that it feels like it will most certainly kill you with its intensity. From the unnoticed and incomprehensible fear of something inside you that prevents you from doing what you need to do to succeed, to the soul-scorching terror of having your throat slit. We are learning that that in modern society our natural and good instinctive fear of being killed has been twisted to suit our times. Now our fears of failure, emotional pain, and a myriad of other intangible things have produced the greatest incidence of "mental illness" ever seen on this planet. Anxiety disorders, panic attacks, Complex Post

Traumatic Stress Disorder (C-PTSD), toxic procrastination; all of these things leading mainly to the destruction of self. Worse than having these things so hugely and negatively affecting our lives is that we don't understand what is happening to us, and because of the stigma attached to "mental illness" we fail to seek help. We consciously hide what is killing us due to another fear—fear of ridicule—and so it grows, and sinks its dark tendrils deeper within us, until we come to believe that maybe the only relief from it could be death.

Fear is the greatest contributor to our shadow, and one of the greatest, yet most difficult to admit to, is our fear of shame—ridicule. We instinctively fear being seen as weak. Weak members of the social herd (and humans are a social herd) in the wild are not respected—they are cast out. These instincts are still alive and well in humans even though we no longer live in caves, but because our challenges are not in the hunt or in our physical strength, the still very alive active parts of our ancestral brain tries to learn from the things that have hurt us in the past. We learn to fear what we perceive to have caused these hurts. Sometimes we perceive ourselves to have done this, and live in unconscious terror of our own selves.

Apart from obvious fears such as the fears of heights, spiders, the dark, ghoulies, and so on, clever creatures that we are, we have created a whole lot of amorphous fears—fears that we often don't even know that we have. Inspirational teachers will tell us that some of our biggest impediments to success are our fears of failure and success. Two opposites, yet it is true, we often do fear the repercussions of both. We fear change. Any change. Humans are not fond of change, even if it could be of great benefit to us. Even if our current state is horrible, it is still a state that we are accustomed to. Fear of ridicule is another animal. Our fear of ridicule will stop us from admitting that we have a fear of ridicule, because admitting that would mean admission that we have indeed over the course of our lives been ridiculed, so therefore we have something about us that deserves to be ridiculed. What a terrible admission to make.

Even in loving and stable homes we can teach our children that embracing what they love is wrong. We teach them to fear being different, and when supposedly different wants and needs arise they make us fearful of ourselves and the urges and thoughts that we are capable of. We teach our children to pursue perfection in popular and "acceptable" studies, sports, and hobbies. Artistic and other abilities described as creative are seldom encouraged as something that will support you in your future adulthood. This is not maliciously done in most families. They're just looking out for your success in life, and everyone knows that creatives and artists starve, right? It is true that only few of them ever rise to the top, but that is the case in most careers. There are lots of regular jobs for creative people out there. Apart from that you could have been brought up in an abusive environment. A childhood where the adults and caregivers in your life were intentionally hurtful to you. There is not much harder than overcoming the terrors instilled in childhood by adults who got their jollies from bullying the only people in their environments who truly couldn't get away from them.

Fear of ridicule is an overlooked factor in both the fear of failure and the fear of success. What is the worst thing that could happen if you fail? You could lose respect. Your attempts could be seen as futile. You could appear as "less than able". What is the worst thing that could happen if you succeed? You could be seen as "different". You would have separated yourself from the pack, and you could be alone in your success. We will do pretty much anything to stay within the safety of the pack, and so this one fear is one that we must work much harder at to overcome.

Part of the power that fear holds over us is our reluctance to accept our own singularity. We want to feel part of something rather than to feel alone. We expect things from others whether we admit it to ourselves or not. And we blame others for not giving us things that we could very easily give ourselves. We make excuses for not doing what we know will be best for us by blaming others for robbing us of the ability to do so in one way or another. The truth is that no matter how many people and things we surround ourselves with, we remain unique and solitary within our own bodily worlds. The truth is that we can *be* anything we choose to be regardless of what anyone else has done to us or not done for us. And yet fear freezes us. We are terrified to try. We can *choose* to not try anything because of the fears we mistakenly believe are insurmountably part of who we are because of the actions or inactions of others. We can also *choose* to give what we desire our best shot regardless of the fear. Even though these things are true, they are hard truths to completely embrace and live by, especially when fear has had years to settle in—to sink its roots into the dark recesses of our inner selves, and when we still believe that the only way to avoid the terror is to run from it or avoid it.

I am somewhat of an expert on fear. It's not nice to admit that you've lived most of your life in terror of some thing or another, but for me that was a truth. It is not true anymore, but the memories of it are very clear. There were times when my fear could have been called reasonable, but in hindsight I can now tell you without any shadow of a doubt that while *fright* is sometimes useful, ongoing fear *never* is. I was afraid of quite a lot growing up. I don't recall a single night that I wasn't afraid of going to sleep in the dark, so I used to stick my head under a pillow and wait until I couldn't physically stay awake any longer and passed out from exhaustion. Things that happened— pretty constantly—taught me that life was indeed something to fear, and that continued non-stop into adulthood. Eventually I cracked and ended up stuck in a permanent state of panic. I'm not fond of medication unless I have absolutely no choice, so I looked for help elsewhere—inside of me—and I got it. I was fine for quite a while, and then more happened.

I have had several attempted home invasions. The first time they tried to rip a security gate from its hinges. Fortunately it held at the lock and all they did was make a racket. Closer inspection revealed that they had first tried to force windows, and the sight of that mangled and bent gate, as well as the footprints in the sand all around the house was terrifying. They came back and made off with a laptop. Shortly after that my husband passed away, and while I was alone in the same house they came three times more—that I knew about—once I actually came face to face with one trying to get into my office window. Sleep and peace departed until I moved.

More recently there have been three more terror inducing incidents. Living on a remote farm in a flimsy walled pair of rooms quite a distance away from any other people in South Africa is probably not a great idea in these times. These times these intruders did indeed get in and manage to steal quite a lot—once again not directly into those of us living there's rooms, but they did leave a bloody splodge on the wall a few centimetres from my door where one of them had stood and clearly considered trying to get in. It was enough to instil fear into most hearts. It was clear that they were prepared to do a lot to get what they wanted. The lonely remoteness of the place meant that help would not be forthcoming in good time, and that should they actually get hold of a living resident, they would be able to do pretty much what they wanted to. The reality of the farm and home invasions in this country over the past years is filled with death and torture. Quite inventive torture. Octogenarians have been slowly and painfully killed using only scalding water poured over their bodies from a repeatedly boiled kettle, or being subjected to the constant placement of a red hot iron all over them until they literally died from these injuries, and much worse. There is lots of racial hatred in this country, so that is a factor also. So, yes, I was very afraid. I would force myself to go to sleep at seven in the evening so that I could wake at midnight. I thought that they wouldn't try and get in before then.

I finally figured out that I was wrong. So I armed myself, alarmed points of entry, and made sure that anyone who did make it through the door would have a rather nasty surprise in store. I slept peacefully from then on. You can never guess what any other person or creature will do with any degree of accuracy. Therefore fearing what might happen is absolutely pointless. Obviously I'm not suggesting that you don't consider any horrible thing that has a high possibility of happening to you, but *only* in the context of what you can do to prevent, avoid, or overcome it, and not in fearful imaginings of scenarios that may or may not ever happen. This applies to physical danger, emotional pain, lack of anything that you need, or any other thing at all.

Physically fear, no matter what the perceived source, will keep you awake when you should be resting. It will elevate your cortisol to dangerous or even life-threatening levels. It will damage your organs—your heart and your brain will take a hammering, and you could find yourself in such a state of anxiety that you feel that nothing you can do can ever get you out of it. Fear is not easily overcome when you truly believe that you are alone in the world. That there is nobody who will have your back, and that there is nobody who truly loves you. This is why fear is the most powerful tool in the evil arsenal. It is also a very great lie. Not only is there love out there for every single one of us if we're prepared to accept it, there is also incredible power to overcome anything at all that we have to overcome once we realise the reality of this.

Unfortunately our world has moved far away from believing in the reality of the spiritual realm that exists, because we don't learn enough about it to understand the infinite power of tapping into it for help in our everyday lives. Organised religion is often mocked and believers are laughed at for being so gullible. Organised religion is also historically responsible for some of the worst atrocities in human history, and to this day, in the name of whichever name these people assign to what they think is the almighty. People can claim anything they like though, and because of the law of free will and freedom of choice they will not be zapped by divine lightning from the heavens.

It is clear to anyone who does have love in them to see that anyone who blows up whole groups of innocents is most certainly not acting on the instructions of a loving God. We then ask why a loving God would allow such acts to be carried out in His name. Some then reach the conclusion that if these things can happen then there can be no loving God, and so we strongly avoid becoming part of anything remotely religious. We vote to have anything to do with it taken away from schools and public institutions. I do agree that everyone should have the right to choose, and that any belief system should not be allowed to be force-fed to those little sponges that are children. The problem with this is that these sponges are not actually being given the right to choose anything but rather are instilled with the beliefs of their parents. It would be much less destructive to our race in general if all the beliefs of the world were taught as a part of human history, which is indeed what they are. Children should be taught more than what we believe as individuals to be truth so that they can arrive at their own truths. It seems that in all religions at some point there have been groups of leaders in them who have decided which parts of them were fit for human consumption and which parts were not. They removed from their historical texts those things that they decided we could not or should not handle, and that was that. There are some that believe these removals were divinely guided, but I personally prefer to make my own choices while being divinely guided myself. Often information was kept from the population to retain power for the priests, because that knowledge could possibly free people from their control otherwise. Historically many churches have used fear to control their parishioners. Fear of hell. Fear of the wrath of God. Some churches have made quite a lot of money from these fears.

Bear with me once again for a moment while I move into the strange realm of those we see as the crazy fringe people. Those apparent nutters who put forth the conspiracy theories. There is certainly enough to be feared there. It is very unfortunate though that many of these theories stem from actual physical or historical facts, because once these people get done with them, nobody in their right mind will want to hear anything that they spout, so the little nodes of truth at the centre of their theories never get to be properly looked at. This is very similar to those who twist the words of their written religion to justify the vicious extermination of others. There is nothing like a *little* truth to get believers, but then when the unreality of what coats those truths becomes unacceptable to decent humans we turn away from all of it. So we often miss out on the hidden kernels of truth.

I tend not to believe in anything I haven't seen for myself. I've never seen a UFO or the Loch Ness Monster for instance. There have been thousands of hoaxes and faked photographs, as well as stories of alien encounters that have finally proved to have been fabricated. More so than those cases as yet still open for debate. Who would want to be associated with behaviour like that, even if only by admitting to believing that these things could possibly exist? The truth is that, having only one world in the unimaginable expanses of this universe that is or has been home to sentient life is not logical. Until we have proof one way or another we can't say whether or not little green men have been visiting us, and if so, what their motives are. As far as old Nessie goes, it is a fact that there are thousands of yet undiscovered species on Earth and in her oceans, lakes, and rivers. How about those six foot tall tubeworms with blood resembling our own discovered far beneath the sea, where there is no light—where we were previously adamant that no life could exist—living and thriving on volcanic light and energy? There is probably a whole lot of unbelievable to be found in the wild places of our planet happening right now, from the mutated to the as yet unseen. Just because something hasn't been specifically eyeballed by a member of Homo Sapiens does not mean that it doesn't exist.

The reason I mention such particularly "out there" beliefs such as these two things is because in many respects our current world view that everything must be seen to be believed is also responsible for our reluctance to believe in the reality of actual forces in the spiritual realm of both good and evil. It is hard to believe that there are intelligent wills that wish us to fail in every way, and to either commit evil acts or to become so afraid and dysfunctional within ourselves that we will die without ever living up to our potential to live great lives and to have a positive impact on humanity in either small or huge ways. Or if we do believe something similar to this, we don't believe that there are also intelligent and loving wills who are very present and available to help us, guide us, inspire us, and very often to protect us. Once we do realise that we are very much loved, and that the most powerful force in all creation will indeed have our back—once we really, really get that—then fear has little power over us anymore.

Fear is probably the single most damaging emotion in all of humanity. Most bad actions are rooted in fear. Racism, terrorism, murder, misogyny, often even abuse. First, understand that you will always have fear of some kind. It's new every day, and it has to be faced in every one of its incarnations. There is no way to get rid of fear for the rest of your life. Every time it pops up it has be to dealt with, or allowed in to control you and run rampant over everything you are trying to accomplish. That is its job. You will become stronger and stronger with daily practice though, and finally every fear that arrives you will find easier to overcome.

Here is the easy answer to squish fear. Simply realise the truth of the fact that the greater your fear of doing something is, the more important it is for you to do it. Are you afraid of plonking yourself down on the couch with a family-sized packet of Doritos and a big bag of assorted choccies to spend the day watching your boxed set of Lord of the Rings? Of course not. Are you afraid of writing the self-help book you *know* will help loads of people? Of course you are. Even though the fearful thoughts of making a fool of yourself and having the cheek to put yourself in a position to advise other people purely on the basis of your life experience pop up a lot less often when you are banging away at your keyboard than when you are not, they can be strong enough to stop you forever if you let them.

Fear is often the driving force of procrastination, particularly procrastination which will result in harm to yourself in things such as not meeting deadlines, or failing to do anything which would benefit you, financially or otherwise. We can spend hours—days—weeks, even months and years trying to figure out *why* we are doing these self-destructive things. This wondering in itself is just as damaging as the fear, and a very clever trick of your shadow/subconscious. The only solution to this is to do it afraid. Seriously. Sit down and make a later appointment with your fear. Tell it out loud if you have to that you will entertain it at nine o'clock on Saturday evening. Then open your books, switch on your computer, or get out your paper and paints, or whatever else it is that you want to do, and just begin to get on with what needs to be done. Every time you feel a tentacle of fear attempt to rise up, remind it that it has a later appointment, and that you are currently too busy to hear what it has to say. I promise you, the other side of a job done *through* fear will go a huge way to getting rid of it—once the job is done you will realise that the fear was completely irrelevant. When you have your Saturday meeting with fear you can probe for its root, comfort that part of you that bred it, and move on without it. It will come back of course, but after every meeting it will be weaker, and finally you will triumph over that particular fear and move on to your next life project.

This book would be way too thick if it included all the treatments for all the ails that ail us on the road to becoming all that we can be. Hopefully it will help you realise where you need work, and send you further on to each specific area in your life that you want to concentrate on at any specific time. So to help you with those things I will occasionally point you to others who have greatly helped me— opened my eyes when they needed opening, and offered solutions and comfort. Books offering solutions to depression, anxiety and panic attacks are big sellers in this world of ours at this point, and with good reason. There are millions of people on the planet today for whom these things are very real and daily issues in their lives. Nobody wants to wake up every day with sadness and apathy sitting like tiny rocks in every atom of their being, then spend the day with, and go to sleep with these soul destroying companions. Everyone is anxious from time to time—it's natural in small doses, but when it's a constant companion, or when you find yourself terrified of nothing at all, with your cortisol levels through the roof, you're probably going to look for help. Books are cheaper than therapy, and less embarrassing. In fact, some therapists will recommend certain books as part of their treatment. Obviously not all self-help books are equal—a few are downright dangerous and some are mere rip-offs of others, but there are quite a few that will indeed help, and so there is a list of some of those that have helped me very much on my path at the end of this book. Maybe you'll only need to read one to set you on your way, but it is true that one really enlightening book can begin a great journey.

At some point though, you are going to have to do some work, and often that work is going to be difficult. There is no book ever written that has the power to "fix" anyone at all simply by reading it. There is nothing inside you that can be automatically switched from hurting to fabulous simply by the acquiring of knowledge or information. You have to take what you learn from the reading of books that can help you understand what is wrong and how to make it right, and implement what it has shown you. Sometimes what you learn is nothing at all what the book is trying to teach, but that's the beauty of intentional growth and healing. When we make the decision not to be broken any more, good stuff suddenly appears from all sides. We just have to be brave and stay front and centre no matter how scared we are. We have to stay aware—stay *looking at and focusing on our reality, inside and outside*—and that's seldom easy.

Our societies are riddled with fear, and the anxieties that so many live with are not unreasonable. Any truly sane person analysing the world that we live in with all honesty will have no way to state that our societies are conducive to the potential happiness and wellbeing of all. Life choices are limited to the way lives are already being lived when and where we are born, and very few can afford to decide to live differently unless they're prepared to walk a hard road. Expectations are set. What we eat and how that sustenance is come buy are things that are already in place. We might not like these things, but we must either choose to not think about them or run the risk of rocking boats and personal mental and emotional pain considering them. There are expectations of what we will learn and what work we will do according to the "level" of society we are born into, as well as our gender and race. The games we play—the things we do for entertainment—how many children we have and how we raise them— all of these things that we do are factored more by what everyone else is already doing than by what we want to do.

One thing that causes much fear is change. Not so much actual change but rather the fear of the as yet unknown. Yet terrifying change is often a catalyst for something wonderful coming. People don't like it though, and as long as they feel relatively safe in a current situation they are not going to want to change. If they think it's coming they are going to try and avoid it at all costs, and if they can't, they will likely quiver in terror at the thought of the unknown ahead. Humans mostly imagine worst-case scenarios when it comes to great changes. The loss of a job is not going to be a happy occasion for anyone with bills to pay and no money in their bank account. This person would not have resigned. Maybe not, but so many job-losses have been the beginning of wonderful, successful paths for people forced to change. Sometimes a hard change opens doorways to doing what we should be doing—what we will love to do. We finally look back and see that the fear we felt could have overcome us if we let it, and we realise that fear is always much less fearful if we look at it. Just like all the weapons of darkness, when you turn to face them they have a habit of scuttling away.

PEOPLE HAVE SHADOWS

When I first learned that every one of us has a shadow self it creeped me out a little. As if I had just discovered that there was something demonic in me, and that if I were to poke at it in any way it could leap out and possess me. It was only when I realised that it is *inherently human* to sometimes do dark things or have dark thoughts, and that we have choices about how we respond to these things that I realised that our shadow is not to be feared, and that exploring it can be an incredibly joyful experience. Parts of digging in its depths can also be traumatic, so make sure to be properly prepared before you begin, and if you do suffer from severe anxiety, depression, or any other form of fearful or anger issue, please do *first* consult with a mental health professional. Sometimes the company of someone who knows about these things is necessary for when you go rootling around in your hidden psyche.

It is dangerous to deny any part of who you are. To not accept everything that you have done or caused to be done is to deny your own truth—the very being that you are. Some things that we do though are things that we are not proud of. Some things that we do we don't even consciously realise are things better not to have done, but some of our unthinking words or actions have terrible consequences. These are not things that we want to think about or accept that we have done, and so we bury them deep within our subconscious. Then there are the things that happen to us that are horrible in one way or another. The shame and fear we feel as children can cause us to bury good things about ourselves too. Someone criticising a child's creative idea can lead to anything creative being buried. Growing up is a minefield of opportunities to send parts of who we are down into the depths of what is called our shadow.

Good things and bad things go there, sometimes to remain hidden there until we die. That is to be avoided if possible, because owning exactly who we are, warts and all is more than liberating. It makes us whole. We become more self-aware. We "wake up" a little more, and that is pure joy. Going back to what near death experiencers share about their life reviews is that it changes them for the better. They come back wanting to do better, and to be better. Why wait until you die to do that when you can do that now? You can do it regularly, and work on making yourself better and happier while you live.

It is only in accepting the "rightness" of our humanity that we can finally begin to become whole. When we learn to truly love ourselves and be grateful for the perfection and great gift of our own creation that we will stop hurting ourselves. We hurt ourselves more than anything outside of ourselves ever does. The object of "accepting" the shadow is not so much accepting it as *seeing and acknowledging* it. Then either forgiving it and thereby allowing it to exist within us peacefully, or welcoming it as an awake and active part of our current selves.

Thinking that there are various personas lurking within us, some that we are not at all aware of, and others that we would not for a single waking moment wish to be within us, let alone an actual *part* of who we are can sound like something out of a horror movie. It is true though. Various parts of who we are are sent underground during the course of our lives for various reasons, and they stay mostly hidden from our face to face view until they explode out when we least expect such a thing, or we go looking for them, as we eventually must if we want to reach a state of peace—wholeness.

Finding out about the reality of the shadow in each and every one of us is liberating. It's a real and acceptable thing finally. Jung taught of it, but there is not enough knowledge of it these days in general society. Our shadow contains the things that we have repressed during the course of our lifetimes. These are not always bad things.

We bury parts of ourselves capable of creating great beauty and giving ourselves great joy for various reasons. We also inhume those things that we know to be, or are taught are bad, evil, wrong, or unacceptable to society, our childhood caregivers, or those we love and respect as adults. When you are unfortunate enough to have a narcissist abuser in your life you will hide those things that they mock, and they *will* mock all your light, your beauty, your talents, and everything that most others would like about you. Everyone has a shadow within, no matter how much their lives appear to be a fairy tale to onlookers. When we are small we do whatever we have the inclination to do with no thought of wrong, right, or the fact that we might get hurt. Acting in ways that ensure that we don't get hurt is instinctive though, so we learn quickly. We learn to hide our anger, our fear, our grief, and often, our happiness or pleasure. We run from discomfort.

We have all done things that we either knew at the time were wrong, or we know now in hindsight. Even if we didn't intend to do the horrible thing that we did because of uncontrollable emotion, or it was the result of a stupid accident, we still feel bad when the memory of whatever it was intrudes. We get rid of that memory as fast as we can to avoid feeling pain. There is no point in wallowing in self-recrimination about something done that can't now be undone after all. Unless we are truly leaning towards becoming evil we don't want to see anything we've done as evil, because we don't want to be evil, so we just don't look at any acts of perceived evil done by ourselves because somehow we think that the deed makes who we actually are evil. We repress the feelings that led to the act. Fear, anger, jealousy, or rage. We try and stop these feelings from happening. We can squish these emotions for years. But not forever. When they've been repressed, they will come back when you least expect them to, stronger than ever, and lead to actions that can hurt you or others. These are natural feelings, and nothing to be ashamed of. It's not the feeling of them that is bad, it's the way we react to them. When they come, and we should allow them to come, all we need to do is to look at them before acting on them.

It is important to look within, and it is of vital importance that when we do look, we accept whatever we see. Whether we think that what we see is bad, embarrassing, or any other thing, we must accept it unconditionally as part of who we are or were. For instance, you may have acted in a horrible way in your distant past, and naturally you're not going to want to rerun that situation over and over in your head. When good people consider apparently shameful things that they have done, it can hurt a whole lot more than when they mull over the bad things that others have done, either to them or others. What we need to do is to let it come up once and look at it as deeply as we can. For the purpose of understanding, not justification, we must honestly examine the reasons for our actions. While there can be no excuse for harming another, when we lack the self-control of self-awareness we can, and do, do things that we wouldn't normally do without stressors such as badly formed beliefs about ourselves and the world.

So maybe we were filled with bottled up rage at the way we ourselves had been treated. Maybe we were acting in ways that we had been taught were acceptable, such as physical violence or control by threat rather than with loving guidance. As we grow we get to choose whether to continue to act in these ways or not, and when we don't, we sometimes get to experience great remorse and sadness over the things that we did before we chose the paths of empathy. This guilt serves no purpose now, and so we take it up, we examine it, we lovingly forgive our past self, and we then let it float away. We do not shove it back down to fester and damage our soul any further. We let it go away—out of us. A lesson learned, never to be repeated. We understand that we are not perfect, and that that is alright. We love ourselves no matter what mistakes we have made. We learn from our mistakes and move on to new things, letting go of the old, rather than storing them up inside of us where they have the power to pop out unexpectedly and do more unnecessary hurting.

Sometimes when fear is all you know, your strength, courage, and power, are to be found buried in the recesses of your shadow self.

There is much more than dark impulses and shameful secrets lurking in our shadow. Some of those things that we loved but couldn't have because of some perceived fault in ourselves, or responsibility that made that love too expensive to partake in, we buried too. So as well as concealed rage or fear, you will find joy bubbling up also when you work on exploring your shadow.

Each one of us is born unique. No two people on the planet have exactly the same temperament, talents, or weaknesses. During the course of our lives we "learn" that some of these things are either "good/useful" or "bad/useless". Maybe a well-meaning parent will suggest that we follow a *sensible* course of study rather than one we love, and so we completely cut out the thing that we love from our hearts and thoughts. Or so we believe. Also, we all have an innate set of values. Things that we don't approve of. When we ourselves step over the line of what is acceptable to our core self, then we create a conflict that sometimes cannot be resolved within. The who that we are cannot condone or accept a certain behaviour or action that we have committed. We refuse to accept that piece of ourselves as part of ourselves, and it gets "torn off and sent away". It becomes shunned by ourselves. We don't look at it or accept that such a horrible thing is actually us—part of who we are. And yet it is.

Say that when you were six years old an abusive father beat you to ribbons for answering back. That teaches you that you do not have the right to defend yourself, and that others can and will hurt you badly for trying to. Standing up for yourself gets consigned to the bad box. Maybe as a small child you reacted in anger when your hamster bit you and you reflexively hit it hard enough to kill it. This led to you being told that you were an evil little sod by your brother, and advised not to tell your parents the truth. This teaches you that "you" are bad, and that you must keep your badness secret. That belief in your own personal badness would then mean that you were in actual fact not even good enough to process the grief that you felt at the loss of your pet. So grieving goes into the bad box. Maybe if you had told your parents they would have gently showed you that hitting is always bad, but that your hamster's death was not due to you killing it with forethought and on purpose. You would instead have learned that you will make mistakes in life—sometimes grievous mistakes— but that they didn't make "you" evil, and you would have begun the journey to learn how to deal with anger when it arrived rather than acting out on it without thought. This one act and the consequences of it could have consigned far too much to the shadow.

The little frustrated artist, the child that spoke back, and the child who loved animals before he "learned" that he was an evil killer will still reside in you though. I don't mean this in a creepy multiple personality way, but even though we change throughout our lives because of our experiences, the whos that we have been don't ever leave us. They are not always bad whos either.

Shadow work shows you how to love yourself exactly as you are, with all your loves and foibles. You begin to care for yourself and to like yourself. You begin to enjoy life and finally allow yourself to have a little fun. Imagine for a moment that what some people who have had near death experiences say is true. The bit about having a life review after dying. They say that you see everything you've done throughout your life—good and bad—and you experience the effects of your actions on yourself and others. It sounds pretty grim for people who have lived thoughtless lives, but basing your shadow work on this process is very helpful. You don't have to try and feel the effects of your actions—just dive into the memories of your life that you never consider, going as far back as you can because some of our deepest injuries occur very early in life. Our shadow begins to form at birth. Some of this will be difficult and some will release fabulous parts of you that will change your life. Good or bad, digging these things out and inspecting them, and then owning every single one of them, will chase away many wrong beliefs you have about yourself and your life that underlie your fears, habits, and behaviours without you having a conscious inkling of it.

If you refuse to accept who you are, or even to admit to who you are, you are going to be a stuck puppy. Being a self-perfectionist is going to hurt you, and refusing to let go of the things you have (or believe that you have) done in your life will prevent you from becoming the best that you can be. We allow so many things to prevent us from being kind and loving to ourselves. Super empaths who pretty much will do anything for anyone, and constantly dole out love and pieces of themselves to others for zero compensation can be the nastiest people when it comes to dealing with themselves. Merely considering treating another the way that they often treat themselves would be appalling to them.

People are taught to be humble. Nobody likes a blowhard constantly telling the world how great they are. That is good. Don't be a blowhard. But don't deny what is good about yourself, or your talents and abilities, especially to yourself. If you are a good writer eventually you will find out that that is a fact. People who don't know you or love you will read what you write and they will say that they love it. When this happens over and over, you have to accept that what you wrote that they read was good writing. You generally figure out at some point what you are good at. It is something that you love to do. If you paint a beautiful picture you should be able to see that. Unless you really are a blowhard and are fooling yourself, in which case others will eventually help you understand that your strengths do not lie in art. But they do lie somewhere. Everyone is good at something. Sometimes that something is waiting for you in your shadow.

Occasionally you will know that something you have done or want to do is good and nobody will agree with you. Nobody will buy it. Why is that? It could be that you are wrong but that is unlikely to be the case. When we feel so strongly about something being good and needed, what mostly stops us is our own inner resistance projecting outwards from our shadow, stopping our success by telling us in no uncertain terms that we are in fact no good. What we want to give or sell that we think is good or needed is deemed to be sub-standard by our resistance. It is a powerful force in every one of us that mostly wins, and talents, beauty, genius ideas, and words or things that could have had huge impacts on the world fade away to nothing.

When you accept the "bad' in your shadow and joyously find the hidden good bits, you don't have to rush around telling whoever will listen to you how fabulous you are, but always accept within yourself all the good that you are and all the good that you can do. Never belittle yourself or your talents and abilities within or without. Being honest with yourself and about yourself should never be a long list of all your failings, which is usually the kind of self-talk most of us partake in. Being honest about the fact that you are indeed a nice person, a brilliant mathematician, cook, designer, or cleaner is essential not only for your spiritual wellbeing, but also the first rung towards any sort of success in the "real" world. The people who started hugely successful cleaning businesses were not ashamed of "only" being good at cleaning. They took that apparently humble talent and turned it into success. No good thing or talent is humble. These things are great gifts and talents, and it is important that we are grateful for them, and kind to who we are. Now is the time to stop running away from your shadow.

PEOPLE HAVE PURPOSE

Not everyone believes that there is any purpose at all to our lives. I get that. It took me totally (if incredibly sadly) accepting the fact that there was no purpose at all to my existence to suddenly find that I did indeed have a purpose. Even if that purpose was simply to try and achieve what *I* wanted. We all have a purpose. It is natural for people to consider what is in it for them before they take on their life's work. Unfortunately in modern society earnings have to be taken into account in a big way because unless you already have enough money to live on you can't spend all your time doing what you want to do. Then there is the age old question—but what if this is all there is? I asked the same question, and the answer came to me immediately— so what if it is? Followed shortly by the thought that it makes no sense that the life and the beauty of this world is accidental. I knew at once that what I wanted to do was help those wronged and to bring the balance on this planet up for good—even if only by the measurement of a small grain of sand. My gifts and my experiences allow me to try, and try I want to, and so *voila* I have a purpose. Evil and good are a fact of life, and so for those still hanging on to the belief that this is all there is, what is the harm in choosing sides and leaving a better place behind us when we do die here? Having said that, I personally do believe that this is most certainly not all there is. I also do not believe that every one of us has to have some lofty purpose. We all need goals to live fulfilled lives, and what is a goal if not a purpose? No matter how small or large, every goal is a purpose.

Even though I now believe that we all have a calling on our lives, it would be a mistake to think of one calling more noble than another. Maybe your calling is teaching ballet, or being a wonderful caregiver, or maybe it's cleaning houses. You don't have to win a Nobel prize to find your true path in life. You never know who you "touch" while carrying out your work, nor do you know how much of an impact that touch will have. I have been deeply inspired by several people who have never even heard of the notion that people could have any small or great purpose to their lives. One of them was a domestic worker. A simple, poor woman who spent her whole life struggling to make ends meet. She believed in corporal punishment, and when all there was for her family to eat was a small bowl of dry porridge, she'd clout any whiners on the ear and tell them to eat it or leave it, because that was it. But her heart was filled with love. She couldn't read, and she had no especially noticeable talents, but she would take the shirt from her back to give to a beggar, and she had a love that emanated from her so strongly that it was almost visible. She gave people love and comfort when they needed it, and they were helped by it, smacks on ears notwithstanding. That to me was evidence enough that she was living her calling in life.

Humans place high value on the respect of others as well as on financial success. We are all born with different talents and desires. We respect people with great talent when those talents are easy to find on display and see, such as in popular music, art, writing or those who use some need to fill a gap and make a lot of money from doing that in the business world. I used to find that a little unfair. I've met people working "humble" jobs who have far greater talent than many I've seen who have attained fame and fortune. Mostly these talents are never seen, and these people get on with making their minimum wages without getting the respect that they deserve—they often get no respect at all because their "value" is judged according to who they are, where they come from, what their day jobs are, and how much money they have in the bank. People are funny that way— it's amazing how the level of respect a floor sweeper usually gets will change if he wins a couple of million bucks on the lottery, and yet he is exactly the same person.

We all leave some kind of legacy when we die. Sometimes it's a great legacy that lasts for generations, and sometimes the only memory of us is in the rat in the corner that watched you die in an abandoned building, all alone and stoned out of your mind. It is wonderful when we are remembered with joy, affection, admiration, and love. I have known people who died leaving only relief at their passing behind. Tyrants who used their intelligence and abilities to boast, love only themselves, and bring everyone around as far down as they could because they imagined this would make them more impressive. They only impressed themselves unfortunately, and I am sure that they are no longer impressed now as they reap what they have sowed.

Other than the main purpose for all—exerting our freedom of choice throughout our lives— and choosing sides, good or evil, everyone has a purpose for their lives. It might be something that comes easily to them, such as being the most wonderful mother to someone special, or it might be that they should be a great teacher to many growing minds. Sometimes our purpose is to overcome seemingly insurmountable obstacles, or survive some terrible trauma, to learn, and so that we can help others on the same scary pathways in their own lives. Fulfilling our life purpose is not something all will achieve.

It seems to me that the greater your purpose is to the benefit of others, the greater will be the resistance you get to doing it. Here's where good and evil come into play. Two certain ways of knowing that you're on the right path to fulfilling your purpose are firstly a feeling of joy when you're doing it, and secondly the size and apparent fearsomeness of the obstacles in your way. Evil has a job to do—to stop you from doing what will make you and others better. Good has a job to do—to guide you with love and cheer you on, no matter what stumbling blocks the bad guys set before you. But good will still allow you free choice. You can stumble if you choose to. It's important to remember that while knowing that you can forge ahead also—if you choose to.

It took me a long time before I realised that fulfilling your purpose doesn't mean that you have to suffer for it, although sometimes suffering can lead you to finding it. Mostly it's as simple as identifying what you love to do or feel very strongly about. It takes courage to share such things sometimes, especially if what you share is something born in the recesses of your heart. This is where fear will stop most of us from starting. Fear of failure, ridicule, poverty, success. No matter how evolved we believe we are fear is hardwired into our genes.

When most of what you've got during the course of your life is pain no matter how hard you tried to get everything right, then you are certainly going to have more than a normal portion of fear, and unfortunately these are the cases where you have to overcome it to have any kind of happy, and because hurting people are not only more likely to hurt more people, but hurt people who face their fears and live good lives, striving to be all that they can be regardless of their terror, make the best teachers for those who might never step on that narrow path to a purposeful life without the inspiration of those who have already faced their demons and won.

Whatever you feel drawn to do, *do it*, do it afraid if you have to, but always strive to live a life of purpose. Try not to waste your time here—whether it's a one off shot or you get to try again with another life at another time. Living your calling is not going to be unicorns and rainbows all the way. The reason we so admire the people who succeed at this is because we know that anything of value doesn't usually come free. You have to put in the work—go without whatever needs to be gone without—take chances. The fabulous thing about this is that once you start the journey of your true calling, God, or the universe, or whatever you call the great love that created everything, will be right there to help you, but always remember that the greater the purpose the greater will be the resistance.

Expect that evil will fight you, and still walk on through whatever it throws at you. Even though you can be sure it's not going to let you go easily after having you afraid for most of your life, you can be sure that things are generally never as frightening as we imagine them to be, and looking right at them diminishes their fearsomeness. That's the truth about most of the things we fear. Look right at them and they shrink. One nice thing to know about evil is that no matter how scary it can get it can never defeat you when you *really want* to win. It tends to sidle away like the coward that it truly is when it sees the glint of faith in an eyeball.

Many people never seem able to find their purpose in life. Then there are those who don't believe in callings or purposes. Some are too busy just keeping their heads above water to find the time to consider the point. Most of us want to know why we are here though. The reason for our human existence remains elusive, if there actually is a reason other than the random coming together of atoms. Ever since mankind has been able to wonder he has wondered why. As our societies continue to become more difficult for more people to function in happily this question is often added to another—why must we suffer so much? People lose hope and they lose faith in the face of what is being done collectively on this world. What purpose could there possibly be in this mess? How can my purpose be to be an artist when that won't stop hunger, war, poverty and pain? What is the point in even trying?

The truth is that it is precisely because of the chaos and pain we see all around us that we must hold on to our hope and our faith. We must strive to make our impact on this Earth we find ourselves on the best one that we can. Everything that comes into being makes an impact, be it huge or small. Every living creature makes an impact. We, who are able to make the biggest impact on our world and every life on it, hold in our hands the ability to make our impact better than it has been. We do not have to join together and wipe out all the bad people. That would merely continue the destruction of ourselves and everything else that humanity seems incapable of not continuing towards. We do not have to continue the way that we have been, even though at this point change seems overwhelming. It seems overwhelming because every part of the way we feel that we have to live our lives seems entrenched. Yet every action that makes this a better world, no matter how small, serves a much greater purpose.

No matter how disastrous you feel that your circumstances are, every second gives you another opportunity to begin to change them. The problem with most of us is that we don't want to begin anything, especially anything important or difficult, unless we know for certain what the outcome will be, and that that outcome will also be good. So we try and be the best that we can be at easier things than the things that we were made to be doing. It's not true that doing what we were made to do will be easy. It is easy to figure out what we were made to do though. That thing that you love to do—the thing that makes your heart sing. That, or something to do with that is what you were made to do. Your purpose.

"God made me fast, and when I run, I feel His pleasure."

Eric Liddell (Chariots of Fire)

Persevere in finding your purpose. It might be that what you love to do might require a little education. Gifted musicians must learn and practice scales, which is not a lot of fun at the time, but necessary for them to finally be able to share their talent. What they produce without this education could be a horrible cacophony. That's where we fall down. That talent is in there, and always will be, but we need to learn how to translate it into something real. Talent is ephemeral. The gift is in seeing the finished result, but we must be taught the technicalities. The most gifted author must learn language—he must learn how to put the words singing in his heart on paper. He must understand grammar—at least the basics. A painter must understand colour, depth, and shading. Lots of genius is lost to the world because people believe they should be born with the ability to create the magic in their minds without any sort of training. Finding your purpose is a journey.

When there is something that we love to do it is important to do it. I'm not suggesting telling your boss to take a hike and your wife to get used to couponing. I'm suggesting starting small. Start learning what you need to know. Figure out the nuts and bolts. While you're doing that, enjoy it. Embrace your incompetence as you struggle to learn how to actually bring your vision to life. We all have different callings, and these callings are made clear to us by the gifts that have been given to us. Most often we use these gifts in creating abundance for others rather than ourselves. Use your gifts to find your purpose and live for yourself.

PEOPLE THINK THINGS

There are a couple of contradictory beliefs in the world of spiritual self-help. One is that nobody gets to escape their karma, and the other is that everybody can have whatever they want if they only believe it. I do go on, quite a lot, about the need to be positive and the fact that dwelling on unwanted outcomes will often get them for you. I say often because the truth is that I have met a whole lot of incredibly negative people who are also incredibly "lucky". They anticipate the most awful things happening to them and somehow the opposite of these things happen to them in actuality. I've also met people who would go to any length to find the good in any situation. They visualise and truly believe in the blessing and abundance that is on the way to them—and it never comes. In fact, sometimes it seems that the universe is having a huge laugh at their expense, and the more they believe the more rotten happenings are piled around them.

That's not to say that your words can't harm or help you. If you not only focus on positive things but take positive actions "luck" is a whole lot more likely to find you. On the other side of the coin the ability of some words to harm you is pretty obvious. For instance, if you're saying horrible things about your boss and he comes in and hears you, you are very likely to be jobless shortly. The main key has a lot to do with what you *do* following your positive or negative thoughts and beliefs. Daydreaming about tooling around in your new Mercedes while never getting out of bed is really unlikely to ever get you a new car of any kind. Focusing on negative thoughts will undoubtedly harm you though, especially if you stay firmly wedged between your sheets. Saying horrible things about anyone even if they never find out about it will hurt you as well as their reputation. That's not to say that when you need to get a truth known in order to protect yourself or another from harm, then you might be obliged to tell of horrible things at the expense of someone who inflicted, or plans on inflicting them. Sometimes we know things about people that are not particularly nice—things that they have said or done that are generally frowned upon by "normal" people. We don't have to share these things, and when we do it for no other reason than to hold an interesting conversation, we let ourselves down more than any other thing. So, don't be unkind—we all make mistakes.

Everyone's heard of the law of attraction. It works in more ways than simply getting all the wonderful things that you *think* that your heart desires. Remember that sometimes your true heart's desire might not be at all clear to you yourself. It will also give you some pretty bad things if you believe that they're coming your way, no matter how unrealistic those thoughts are. Your faith is only as strong as your deepest belief. You can walk around all day muttering positive affirmations, but if you don't one hundred percent believe, you are not likely to get what you're muttering for. I am not an expert on the law of attraction insofar as sticking pictures of BMWs on your wall and visualising yourself in one will get you one is concerned. I prefer to wait and see what fabulous thing is in my future rather than possibly limiting a grand possibility to a vehicle. Personally I found that working on my shadow self and growing in love and respect for myself was the catalyst to good things beginning to pour into my life. I anticipated not a single one of them, nor would I ever imagined them, but come they did, and it was directly from my beginning to be kind to myself and acknowledge that I deserved great things just as much as anyone else. I became open to receiving these great things. And there, I think, is where we can use this powerful universal law to good or bad effect, because what we believe becomes our truth. Visualising anything while not *truly believing* it could be yours is not likely to work, while firm belief itself raises the bar substantially.

There are famous gurus who staunchly believe that we alone are responsible for creating our reality, from the blades of grass we walk on to the sizes of our bank balances. When I've been asked where my inspiration for my fiction comes from, I've often thought that somewhere out there in one dimension or another, everything that can be thought of—*is*—that every scene played out, and every creature or world imagined lives somewhere or somewhen, and that writers are mere receptacles for the thoughts of those who live in these fabulous places. This is a lot less frightening than believing that everything *we* think or imagine pops into physical reality somewhere. If that is truly the case then there are a lot more terrifying things out there than sparkly vampires, given the human propensity for imagining cruel, dark, evil, creatures, scenarios, and acts.

Our words can be equally damaging, even when we think that they're harmless. Sometimes we'll say something to appear humble, and even if we don't start out believing what we say, our words become our truth. Success stories in life don't include parts where success comes from calling yourself a loser, a coward, an addict, or any other horrible thing out loud all the time. Most success stories include the opposite. I don't believe that what you get in life is all down to your thoughts, words and beliefs, because I do believe that we all have a destiny, and that destiny will try and happen no matter what we do, say, or think. I do believe that when we acknowledge and lovingly accept ourselves that we allow that destiny to happen, and also by being in a positive and loving state will attract any amount of great things without you having to name them. We have to understand also that receiving anything, whether it is money or anything else, is not selfish, greedy, or evil. Sometimes it is, but in those cases the selfish, greedy and evil tend to have no problem acquiring it. It is the people of the world who feel guilty having it when elsewhere in the world others have nothing to eat, let alone money. The huge truth that we must all realise that with more loving people having huge amounts of money and power, we will see more good works being done, and less of the tiny portion of humanity that is hanging on to unimaginable amounts of wealth without giving a hoot for anyone or anything else.

If you have any thoughts of being undeserving, then nip those thoughts in the bud. Love yourself and open yourself to receiving bountiful amounts of everything you need, and more, if only so that you can help others to do the same. One of the reasons that people stop short of embarking on big dreams is the fear of embarrassment if they fail. If the dream is particularly big then just wanting it seems unobtainable and therefore a silly notion. People don't like to seem silly, even to themselves. Look at the power of the placebo effect and it becomes reasonable to expect result to follow belief.

PEOPLE RUN AWAY

There is no way to begin this chapter without mentioning that procrastination nearly destroyed me completely. I mean seriously destroyed, terminated, living under a tree with a shopping cart for company kind of damage. It almost won until I discovered that there is a trinity of dangerous instincts that are built into our brains that are meant to ensure our survival, but in the modern world can guarantee our downfall. I learned about the fight or flight response and how it could immobilise you first. The freeze response came as a surprise, and much later on my journey. Even though I knew I could do a certain project with joy and little effort, the thought of beginning it would terrify me—not for any logical reason—the thought of starting would just bring a great sense of discomfort—and a pervading, paralysing, fear that I could not understand. With the knowledge as my main awareness, that my own lack of action would without any doubt ensure my failure, I failed to do what I knew I could easily accomplish.

Once again I bought self-help books. I attended online workshops and seminars. I sort of "got" the message, but it just did not sink in enough to change the way I was behaving. I would literally do anything other than what I knew I had to do in order to pay my bills. I learned about my inner child. I was informed that I needed to love my inner children into wholeness and then everything would be hunky dory. It was not until I got so frustrated that I really wanted to slap my inner child that I realised that more work would be required.

Then I found Stephen Pressfield's book *The War of Art*. It is a fabulous eye-opener, and I highly recommend it. At the time I was sceptical of his suggestion of a real outside force that works very hard to make us fail at creative pursuits—and by creative I mean anything that could benefit humanity—be it intellectually from a finely woven piece of fiction—spiritually, scientifically, medically, something simply beautiful—or just something that could help yourself. I learned better. Now I believe it without any doubt in my mind. The funny thing is that when you do realise that the more resistance you face to getting anything done the more important it will be either to you or others, it suddenly becomes easier to overcome it. It's a lot easier doing battle with something that you know wishes you harm than with yourself.

The more important an activity is to the evolution of our soul, the more Resistance we will feel to it.

Stephen Pressfield

A normal reaction to resistance is to, obviously, procrastinate. The next normal reaction is to beat yourself up about it. You're lazy—you're useless—you'll never get anywhere in life—you may as well give the whole thing up. This almost guarantees that you will indeed fail to complete your project. On the other hand if you react with, "This invisible sod really doesn't want this book/painting/online course/catered meal/anything that will pay your bills/anything that will make you physically, mentally, or spiritually healthier, to be finished by me, so I'm going to do it anyway!" That voice in your head trying to get you to play Candy Crush® or go lie on the couch will scuttle away smartly when you sit down and start. It works *every* time. Just sit down, put the oven on, smile at a customer—whatever it is that you *really* do not feel like doing right now—just start doing it, and you will see the resistance slink away like the much weaker than *you really are* thing that it is.

When it's winning it will instil fear in you, and as we know, fear is the most powerful tool it the evil kit. Fear will make you run from things that will benefit you or mankind. Remember at those times that there aren't only bad guys out there wanting you to fail. There are many good guys right there by your side waiting for you to choose them. They will inspire you and give you strength to finish what you need to finish. Your muse will squish resistance when you do that first thing—afraid or not—and if you can't stop the fear then do it afraid—then the fear will leave. I'm not trying to give the impression here that this is easy—it most certainly is not, but even if you only get going after weeks of doing anything but the thing that you need to do, the important thing is that you did get going. Even if you've put your labour of love on the back burner for the last ten years that doesn't mean it's over. All you have to do is start—work afraid—work when the whole world is trying to get you not to.

If we look at the world and the universe we see that if there were no opposite forces things would simply stagnate. Just so with ourselves, without challenges and problems—even pain—in our lives we would have no need to change and grow, and no opportunity to become stronger, more resilient, and more wise. Having fun is wonderful, but living in a constant state of joy is not going to teach you compassion, patience, humility, and determination. If we face what is when it is awful with a view to making it right, then fear can be replaced with intent, logical thinking, and action. This is something that we must especially strive for when the same problems keep on reappearing in our lives in different forms but playing the same tune. This is obviously something that we *have* to overcome or it will not go away—a life lesson. This is when we have to work through something, afraid if necessary, and fix what is broken within and so attracting bad things from without.

This is a wonderfully interesting area for pondering, and a very dangerous one too. My mother often said that we were "born to suffer" and many times I found that a "safe" haven to run to rather than face up to life's problems and to try and figure out ways to overcome them. Accepting all the bad without question. Taking karma to the max if you will. If you believe in certain schools of teaching of reincarnation you may believe that you (your soul) has chosen a life of terrible suffering because of something nasty you got up to in a previous life. Some would see this as simply that, therefore you deserve to suffer so you may as well just take it on the chin. There are also beliefs floating around that you must pay for the sins of your fathers. In Christianity there is a thing called a bloodline curse. All very scary and demoralising if you take these things to heart at face value.

While I don't entirely agree with these things, I do feel that they are relevant in other ways. We are the products of our ancestry, and there is a lot more that is stamped into our genetic makeup than blue eyes or a propensity for excessive alcohol consumption. We inherit more things than we realise from our parents. We can also genetically inherit their fears. Consider the importance of the microbiome and the physical connections to mental issues, as well as the newly discovered facts about the "feelings" and "instructions" of various organs in our bodies, including our hearts. Just like baby crows instinctively perceive a very particular person as danger when they have never seen him before, but he once tried to hurt their parents, we inherit "warnings" of danger in our very DNA. That is a bloodline curse indeed. Even so we can overcome these things also. It is the very things that we avoid that can teach us the biggest lessons.

PEOPLE BELIEVE

What do you believe life is all about? Have you ever reached a point where you wonder what the point of it all is? All the suffering. More proof of evil than of good. No tangible evidence that your life has any meaning. No tangible proof that you don't simply disappear forever when you die. I have. Several times. Two things that do indeed have tangible proof are the impact that humans are having on this world and on each other. There are many negative things—many more negative things than positive things. But the positive things are what I choose to focus on, and hope that in some small way I can help to prevent more negative things. Even if I can help prevent one negative thing simply by not doing it myself, then I have helped this world.

I know that it is trite to tell people that there is always someone worse off than they, but not only is this true, it is also a great reason to put on some warrior pants and turn our focus elsewhere to help in any way, no matter how small you think that it is. No matter what the great truths of existence are, or even if there aren't any great truths, we get to choose how to live our lives. We can choose to sink into a pit of despair at the horribleness of our reality. We can choose to stay there. Or we can choose to claw ourselves out of there and find out how wonderful it is to focus on a need greater or lesser than our own. It might seem impossible, and it might be the hardest thing you ever do, but I promise you that it will be worth it.

There is honour in baby steps when they are hard to take. This journey—this life—can be very hard for some. Sometimes when serious depression is involved just getting out of bed in the morning seems like an insurmountable obstacle. I know. I've been there. I've also been at points when I've read a book telling me how to get out of my hole and why I should, that I've zoomed around for hours, high on the fact that now that I knew what I needed to do it would be done in a jiffy. It doesn't work that way though, and so when I realised how hard the work was going to be the temptation to give up without even trying was huge—many times. There were many days that it seemed to me that giving up was my only course anyway. Dark days that could have lengthened into my forever.

I didn't think that tiny things would be of any use when there was so much that needed doing, and it came as a great surprise to me that merely beginning tasks that needed doing somehow got me a lot of help and blessings from my unseen but very present cheerleaders. Good honours those who try in the face of great adversity, even when those small tryings seem very insignificant to ourselves. When you just get up and begin, even though you are positive that there is no point in trying because you are way too messed up to save, you will find that you get some powerful help on your way to step two.

We all have different levels of strength at different times in our lives. We also have different levels of fear at any given time. Don't believe that you have to finish that project in order to "deserve" help from good and divine sources. It doesn't matter what you feel is wrong with you or your life. All you have to do is take that first tiny step. That step for you might even be something as basic as getting out of bed and having your first bath in a week, or it might be writing the first five notes of a heavenly symphony. The key to getting the help that you need is only to show that you are willing to try. You don't have to promise that you will be successful. All you have to do is begin.

Life is what you make it in the end. You can't do anything to change your childhood, or the things that have already happened to you. Neither bad things or good things. You can do absolutely zero about the things that you have done. Neither good things or bad things. You can do a whole lot for your future though, beginning right now. You do not have to be afraid. No matter what happens, only you control whether or not you will fear. Getting frights is natural, but you can choose to remain frightened or to try and face and conquer what spooked you. You do not have to worry about what will happen when you die. Whether or not you will be punished for doing bad things is a lot less relevant than whether or not you want to do bad things. Intent is key. Belief is key.

If you believe that it is wrong to go around beating people up, why would you want to do it? If you think it is wrong to hurt anything, why would you want to do it? If you think it is wrong to stand by silently while others do things that you believe are wrong, why would you want to do that? Forget about whether or not others say things are wrong, and live according to what you believe. Do it bravely every minute of every day. Be true to yourself.

I wish I could say that I always, or even mostly, get it right. I don't. Sometimes I forget about this world and wallow in self-pity or anger for a while. Sometimes I forget that the smallest things have value that humans know nothing about. Especially the smallest lives. Sometimes I keep quiet when I know my opinion goes against popular belief. Sometimes I do bad. Sometimes I am bad. Sometimes I am unkind. I often take crap, and sometimes I forget to live. Sometimes I forget that I am going to die, and that this moment will never come again. That's alright. I am what I am, and as long as I am trying, I'm alright.

That is what it is to be human. Giving up is a choice. Truthfully, nobody can prove what lies beyond the veil of death. Nobody knows if our choices will have consequences, but wasting precious time wondering if there will be nothing at all and believing that what we do is irrelevant will not change that if it is true. *What we do have is now*. What we do impacts everything and everyone we interact with, regardless of what we believe. We have who we are, and we have all that is around us. That alone is nothing short of miraculous. That is very much the point of it all. Let us make good use of what we have now regardless of the outcome. You may be very happy when you find that you have grown, and learned, and gained immense power purely from being and doing the best that you can, regardless of circumstances and the opinions of others.

There are no easy answers to the questions we have about why we are here, who we are, and why we do the things that we do. There is not one book that will solve all your problems, and no one belief system that can do that either. We must look everywhere, and learn from the inside out. We must learn what is true for us after studying what has been true for others who have gone before us. The truth that we must accept is that our whole lives are a journey, and that no matter how we start out, no matter who or what hurts us out of the gates or later in life, at some point we get to choose who we become. We can become bitter, unkind, terrified, immobile, uncaring, blinkered, or joyful, caring, productive, and as loving as we can be. If we choose to allow what others have done to us to destroy our lives then it is our choice.

It is not easy to stand in the face of fear and negative self-belief, but once we see those things for what they are we get to choose whether or not we will keep them. Some people are very deeply entrenched in these terrible things, and unfortunately some people will live their whole lives without being able to take charge of themselves for long enough to decide to get off that miserable bus. They believe that they have been too badly damaged to even be able to choose. They believe that they are powerless to change, and that they are not truly loved by anyone or anything. They must see that no matter how hard it appears, there is always a choice, and that choosing to be defeated gives the victory to evil. If you allow evil to destroy you and your life then evil wins. They must see that when they do choose not to be defeated, that when they choose good things both for themselves and for others, they will get help.

Free will is a big deal for humanity. Especially when the way others sometimes use theirs impacts on us. When people commit terrible evil we often blame God. Or we decide that because of these things He can't possibly exist, because how could a loving God allow such things. If you think about this a little it becomes clear that if God has given humanity free will, then that is just what it is. We can do whatever we choose to do. Those that choose the dark path will choose to do bad things, but that doesn't mean that those who don't have to accept these things. We have free will too. We have the free will to intervene in the choices of others just as they intervene in the lives of those they hurt, rob, rape, abuse, kill. Accepting that we all have free will does not mean that we have to sit back and allow it all. This world is the home of all who live on it, and we are allowed to try and make it better. We are allowed to be heroes if we choose to try. When we do we might be quite surprised when we see Good in action. When we use our free will for good we very often get big help. Serendipity happens. Miracles happen when we ask for help to do good. We must keep in mind that every living creature is entitled to free will, and that this free will is taken away much too much and in terrible ways. We get to use our free will to improve what we can for ourselves and for those who can't fight back, and those yet to come according to what we come to believe. And so we must choose what we believe wisely, and in the face of the evidence we ourselves have collected.

PEOPLE LIVE, PEOPLE DIE

Most of us avoid thinking of death. Especially our own. We've made death something to be feared. We want nothing to do with it. We hang on to our youth and vitality and refuse to think about it. Old age, illness, the thought of nothingness; these things terrify us. There are many different beliefs about what, if anything, happens when we die. Any "proof" that we have of an afterlife is hearsay, and if we do believe in our essence, or soul, living on, we're likely to pick the scenario that we like best, regardless of whether or not there is evidence to support it.

For most of my life death terrified me. I'd never seen another human being actually die when I was younger but death was something I thought about a lot. My father died when I was six, and although I didn't remember him, my mother certainly did. His being dead tainted her life, and she often railed against God for "taking" him. Then she died when I was eighteen. She didn't go gently. She was absolutely petrified of dying, and her end was a year-long nightmare of pain and screaming misery. I didn't want any of that. Not dying young, and not being eaten alive in writhing agony by cancer—of course I was scared of dying. I had no direction—no focus—no faith in anything. I spent many years after that running. Never sure what I was running from, but I ran anyway.

When I finally experienced death firsthand, I strongly felt the moving out of the body and the being accompanied away of my husband. I got it. I finally really understood that our lives do not end when our time on Earth does. The body we're in is a temporary vehicle for who we are, and who we are moves outward and onward when the body is done. Our spirit doesn't fear death—our body does, and that's probably quite justifiable. Our bodies do most of what they do to stay alive without any active input from us. They have a strong instinct for survival.

Death also taught me that while I am alive I should immerse myself in life. That it doesn't matter how many times I get things wrong or change my beliefs. Each step I take, each experience whether good or bad, either feeds my soul or hurts it. Living is about changing after all. About learning and growing. It's the routes we take that count, especially in difficult times and trials, and the decisions we make that mould who we become. It is good to cultivate a way of life where you never say never. Never say that you will never again do anything or eat anything or say anything. Never become so rigid in your beliefs that you abuse others because of them. I often wonder if sometimes those people who lash out and rage at others for not conforming to their own beliefs are possibly shouting so aggressively to convince themselves that they really do believe what they are promoting. I don't mean that to insult anyone. I used to get pretty vocal trying to get others to see as I saw then.

What is truth for each person is unlikely to remain the same throughout a lifetime. We learn and we grow. We might enjoy eating mushrooms one day and then not like eating them at all. We might tell all who will listen that we will never drink alcohol again, and that anyone who touches the stuff is weak and disgusting only to find ourselves unable to enjoy a cocktail at a party that we suddenly find we really would like to have. Never say never. Not only with the small things. Just because you fervently believe anything from a diet regime to a religious teaching does not mean that those beliefs will not change as you learn and grow in life. Humans crave certainty. We want to know that whatever we do will have a positive outcome. We want to know that the world we live in is a safe place. Without certainty and a feeling of safety many people exist in states of terror of the unknown future that awaits. The truth is that nothing on this Earth is certain. The rich fail in life, and sicken or die just as the poor do. Nothing is ever guaranteed. Nothing except each individual attitude is guaranteed. And it is that attitude that will guarantee how you will feel no matter what happens to you. Live life with an open mind and an open heart. Try to fit as much inquisitiveness, love, and compassion into each day as you can. Dig deep to find the strength you need to get up when you fall, or are knocked down. Live each moment as if it is the most important moment, because it is. While death is inevitable, it is merely a doorway.

PEOPLE SAY AUM

As at 2018 it was estimated that there were more than 4,200 religions in the world. All of them think that they are right, and that they have the answers we need to navigate this confusing world of ours. Many of them believe that not only are they right, but that anyone who does not believe as they do will go straight to hell, or to some version of that terrifying place when they die. Some of them believe that all who don't believe as they do should be assisted to that place as quickly as possible by using bombs, guns, or weapons of mass destruction. Many of these beliefs cause harm and give rise to evil deeds almost beyond belief, in the name of God. Some are more subtle and lead to damage and hurt within—in minds and souls.

Sometimes we can get quite aggressive when we feel that someone is trying to force us to believe what they believe on the strength of interpretations of writings which we are sceptical about. So even though the last thing that I want to do is get up anyone's nostril and cause them to throw this book against the wall, I am going to share what I know—what's real for me. Religion can make people terrified to explore, research, and discover many real and positive experiences and life journeys, not because they are inherently bad, but because they allow themselves to be blinkered and tethered by dogma.

I never went to church as a child, and the only religious instruction I received was at school, which was perfunctory at best. The schools where I grew up were pretty specific in what they taught. There were schools that taught only Christianity, or only the Muslim or Jewish faiths. My school never explained what or why Muslims or Jews believed what they did. It was only as an adult that I became curious about religions and researched them for myself. Religion as it was practiced, and the writings that we are expected to blindly believe flummoxed me. I thought there must be something deeply flawed in me to not just accept as everyone else seemed to. As I said, I have always had a problem with believing in what I cannot see or feel directly, or at least have evidence of that is too direct to be disputable.

I was confused by some of the passages in the Bible. Some of them are confusing. Still, I was informed of their meaning, and I was also informed that God would not allow people to mess with His words. The words in the Bible, as it is, is as God wants them to be according to most. Even if I didn't understand them, that did not mean that they were wrong—thinking that they were was blasphemy. This scared me a little, because in some cases I did indeed think that they were wrong. I did not presume to know what was right, but there seemed to have been a few things lost along the way—missing pieces. Again, when it is considered that the original writings that make up the Bible as it is today were not always found in a complete state, so naturally there would be bits left out. Suck it up—believe that what you see there is all that God wants you to see, and He has divinely arranged for anything else to not be there for you to see. I tried very hard to squash the constantly popping up questions, such as "What about free will and personal discernment?"

Then things started coming to my notice. I would receive arbitrary emails from places that I had never visited or signed up for. Little messages would arrive, all pointing me in one direction. I am not one to ignore synchronicity, because I know that sometimes we need a little help from what we can't see on our way to our truth. And so began years of trying to make sense of it all, and while I still have not achieved that goal, I believe that I am farther along the way than I would have been if I had allowed the fear of burning in hell for researching what we are apparently not supposed to believe in.

You can't convince anyone to believe in God and you can't show what is glaringly obvious to you to people who see things differently and refuse to even look at anything in any other ways. Their reality is real to them. You can try though. What is glaringly obvious to me is that Jesus existed on this world. He is spoken about in many more historical texts than the bible, as are his actions. His miracles are mentioned in Roman manuscripts, albeit not in any affectionate way. It is also glaringly obvious to me that He came to show guide people *away* from organised religion and into personal relationship with a loving God. Yet what many religions have succeeded in doing is putting Him into organised sects by adding to or subtracting from His teachings. He taught love, forgiveness, kindness, respect, and the reality of a loving God, and still humans teach fear, judgement, revenge, and hatred.

Having said that, it is not that all religions and their followers are purposely trying to mislead everyone. Most people who do believe, and feel God in their lives are generally good people. There have been, and still are, too many atrocities committed in the name of one religion or another, and so, not too surprisingly, many people in this world that we live in now avoid any part of any one of the large variety of established groups like the plague. Hatred builds against one or another group and people dig their heels in and demonise anyone or anything to do with it. Within each religion things that are revered in others are anathema to some—to the point where members are threatened with damnation if they don't believe certain things, do certain things, or behave in certain ways. Not too many of us are partial to being bullied into anything, regardless of how fervently the bullies believe that they are right and only bullying us for our own good.

Minds and hearts are firmly closed, and people refuse to even look at anything that their own group's doctrine has made them blindly believe are bad or wrong, if not downright dangerous. This is a shame, because a lot of wisdom has been shared through the ages from many different sources, and the truth is that we really are not likely to get kudos for firmly entrenching any particular belief, no matter how strongly held by others, as our own without a little study and trying to find what truly resonates as good and right with us down deep within ourselves. We must always be honest with ourselves. I don't think that saying that you followed one thing or another because of fear, or peer or societal pressure when you head over to the other side is going to count for much. If we are going to become whole, honest, and true to ourselves, we are going to have to work a little to decide only for our own selves based on what we honestly believe to be truth—whatever that may be.

During my years of researching religion and spirituality I have been regularly blown away by *some* of its relevance to our world today, and how much *some* of it could help us if we would take the time to explore the subject. I have to say here that some obscure or not so obscure "religions" have tenets and teachings that are so insanely terrifying that I find it hard to believe that they find any followers— and yet they do. Most religions though, are trying to teach us to be the best that we can be. It often amazes me how similar many ancient teachings are when their geographical and time origins have been so far apart. When these things were being spoken about and taught we are told that they could have had no access to the peoples on the other side of the globe saying the same things. This brings to mind recent studies that suggest the possibility that the belief in God is hardwired into our brains, and that praying or meditation, which are actually both very similar things, is extremely beneficial physically, mentally, and spiritually. We should think and decide carefully for ourselves, after having a look at the evidence, before we run away from these things.

Even though I believe that creating beauty of some sort for others while we're here is part of our purpose, the main purpose of our human existence can never be how many fabulous physical objects we amass during our lifetimes when all we get to take with us when we go is our essence. That person we become between the time we are born and the time we die, because nobody really leaves in the same condition that they arrive. It stands to reason that the most important building and acquiring we get to do while we exist in our bodies here are not things that can be touched with our fingers, but riches cultivated within. It makes sense that those old wise people who spent lifetimes searching their spiritual selves and realms have just as much chance of being right than anyone who has become "civilised and educated" enough to operate a computer. It seems that the more time we spend concentrating on our own spiritual selves the more truly civilised we become, and those who focus solely on external riches tend to reap harvests of pride and tendencies toward self-gratification rather than love.

We, as a species, have certainly lost the plot. People who rage at God for allowing all the evil that exists in the world today are missing the point. We are free to choose what we do, and what we allow to be done. Apart from actual natural disasters, of which there are surprisingly few if you consider just how chaotic things really could get without some sort of intelligent guidance, all of our troubles have their roots in the actions of humanity. The way we live—where we live—how we live—what we eat—what we like to do—all of these things have contributed to the horrible things that happen in our lives. Pollution, GMO crops, the way we "raise" and "prepare" our meat, the toxic waste we create. Disease, poverty, war, crazy weather and climate change—these are mostly the results of our actions—not God's.

God doesn't make rapists—society does. The way we raise our children and the way we treat each other are choices we make, and even if we personally have not made the bad choices, the bad choices of our fellow humans have bad effects on us. We may be innocent, but if God were to step in and save the result of every bad choice this life would be pointless. We need to begin to collectively and singularly take responsibility for our actions, and take action to change what we have broken rather than blaming it all on God or waiting for Him to head down here in His chariot and fix it all. The world without man is beautiful, including the death in it. There is no entrapment and wilful torture in nature. Death is a stepping stone and has its place—it's not a punishment. It can sometimes be a blessed release from suffering.

Death in nature is not a sign of a mean God either, and neither does the fact that lions kill pretty gazelles justify the killing that we do. We are the only species around here that professes to be fully aware of what is right and what is wrong. We should be learning from the mistakes that we can see and changing our own behaviours, not doing the same terrible things over and over again because "everybody else does it", and most certainly not because wild animals do it. Believing that everything is random and lucky, or unlucky depending on your view, results of a chaotic universe is not logical. There is order in every part of this world in its natural state.

I don't think that we should ever insult any form of true belief in God. I certainly don't think for a single minute that anyone who loves God and doesn't believe that Jesus Christ was God incarnated on Earth will go to hell. You should also not just "believe" anything without doing a little research, so if you haven't actually read the Bible you are not in a position to either believe or not, unless you have had a personal visitation or other strong evidence. The Christian and Jewish Bibles, the Koran, the Baghavad Gita—all the old "holy" books are actually history books. Read them before you call any of them trash or evil. People will say that the Gospels in the New Testament are a collection of folk tales handed down about a good man, and while inspiring, not to be taken literally while they are purported by very many to be eyewitness accounts of actual events. The same events written down by different people, and further written testimonies of those events can be found in obscure texts that have nothing at all to do with Christianity. Jesus Christ is not an imagination.

Some spirituality seems rather dangerous to me. Playing around with séances and ghosts should not be the way we find out about anything. Evil is quite adept at making itself look good—narcissists are a case in point, and whether you open a door for something dark to enter your life on purpose or not doesn't change the fact that the door is open. There is a lot of evidence that things continue to exist in the spiritual realm, but we should be aware that not all of them are friendly. I don't understand why anyone would actively seek them out, just as I don't understand why the people who do believe that UFOs are visiting our world are controlled by superior beings. Anyone who goes to so much trouble to avoid being seen in the light of day is bound to be up to no good.

On the subject of those evil creatures who commit atrocities in the name of religion we have to be very sure that we realise that on some level they must be fully aware that what they are doing is evil unless they are completely insane. Even if they are completely insane, the people who follow them and do their bidding can't all be equally nuts, so most of them must be aware of it and choose to justify their dark deeds because of potential personal gain or fear. Either way—they choose, and I believe that there will most definitely be consequences for them. If we bear in mind that all we get to take with us when we physically die is who we have become while we have been here it makes a lot of sense to be the best that we can, do the best that we can, and help others to want the same if we can. I don't believe that there's a doorman at the pearly gates sending Budhists or Christians or Yogis to hell for the particular way that they worship God. I think that doorman would be much more interested in how consistently you chose the evil over the good when you were *aware of the difference.*

PEOPLE SAVE THE WORLD

Thank God men cannot fly, and lay waste to the sky as well as the earth.

Henry David Thoreau

Nothing physical that we can create can ever come close to what already exists on this world and around it. We can't reproduce the beauty or the power—the life. We like to look at the beauty of creation, and so we leave our safe homes to look at it now and then, or we look at images that others have taken of it, or worse—we capture it and bring it inside of our worlds. Mankind has lived apart from nature for so very long that the thought of the possibility of living in harmony with it seldom occurs to many. Some people never see nature in its original state. They are born in buildings and die in buildings, and in between they move between other buildings in the pursuit of work, pleasure, help, and safety. They don't know or care about the thousands of species becoming extinct every day, because it has no noticeable effect on their lives—yet.

Thank God men cannot fly, and lay waste to the sky as well as the earth.

Henry David Thoreau

We avoid looking at animal suffering or thinking about it because seeing these things is beyond uncomfortable for most of us. We can't tell other people what to do and we can't stop these things, so what is the point of dwelling on them? That does not mean that we approve of animal suffering, and most of us would not intentionally cause it. Or so we allow ourselves to believe. Many famous people have commented on the general inclination of humans to let well enough be. Dietrich Bonhoeffer said, "Silence in the face of evil is evil itself: God will not hold us guiltless. Not to speak is to speak. Not to act is to act."

Some believe that the coming total devastation of our wild places and creatures cannot be avoided. I don't agree. If people begin one by one to change maybe saving the world that sustains us will become popular. Who knows? We do like to follow trends, and this one could be the saving of us. Already we are looking to Mars to try and ensure the survival of mankind if, as is very probable on our current trajectory, Earth experiences a more serious extinction event of some kind. We will probably be clever enough to be able to sustain a portion of our population on a mostly dead planet Earth, but at this point that is still not a necessary future. What is the point in spending billions on terraforming Mars when that money could be better utilised right here trying to save this world? Moving out into the stars to find new worlds after destroying this one is likely only going to result in us killing those new worlds off too.

Even though there is absolutely no doubt that we cannot take a single physical thing with us when we die, we refuse to try and build up the riches that we can indeed take with us. We refuse to grasp the opportunity to learn and grow *within* the beauty of creation, rather than to stagnate mentally and spiritually at the expense of it. We allow the greedy few to rule and destroy our world because it is the path of least resistance. We accept that there are more than enough houses to go around, but that it is quite fine for one person to own ten of them while ten families are homeless. We accept that it is quite fine for billions of tons of food, including billions of tons of "food" animal flesh, to be thrown onto dumping sites every year because of sell-by dates, while billions do not have enough food to eat. This is *our* creation.

Rather than yelling at God for allowing it, we should be using the free will granted to each and every one of us—the free will which has created this abominable system—to begin to free ourselves from it. Baby steps are better than no steps. Talking of babies—every baby born will be born with less freedom as time goes by considering the path that we are currently on. As resources dwindle the divide between rich and poor will become greater. As things are right now middle classes are already more downwardly mobile than otherwise. Do we want to leave a barren and wasted Earth to our descendents? Because that is exactly what we will do if we don't, at least individually, begin to try and change. Not with anger and rage at others who we blame for their part in the horrible wounding of our planet. We need to forgive or we will stoke unnecessary fires, but while we forgive the mistakes done and being done, we must lovingly and firmly work towards healing and safety for all.

We deny the destruction that our "civilisation" has and continues to wreak on this world at our peril. Please don't con yourself with the platitudes of animals killing each other in various horrible ways, or the apparent evil of the snake swallowing the baby bird alive—not to mention things that appear horrific to us, and the "vermin" species such as Cockatoos and the huge flocks of Quelea that we feel that we *must* shoot or poison in their thousands because of the damage they do to our crops.

There is no comparison to the death dealt by the lion or the snake to a slow death by poison, and let's not get into animals raised for meat, skin, feathers, and some of the other apparent necessities to some, such as foie gras. It always amuses me when lovers of the stuff get all hot under the collar about shark fin soup or roast dog. All of these animals die cruel and terrifying deaths after living equally horrible lives. I'm not trying to be holier than thou here—just trying to be logical. I'm as much to blame as anyone else for the torturous lives and deaths of animals even though I wasn't there to see them happen. If we are going to wear, eat, or sleep on something, let's at least be honest about it.

Now to get a little religious. Just yesterday a group of us had a slight altercation about the justification of being paid a huge sum of money for catching and handing over a small animal much prized in the use of extracting oil from it after slaughtering it, which oil is then treated to some African witchcraft ceremony before being sold to guarantee success in business and finance. I'm happy to say that most agreed that they would never do such a thing, not only because getting involved in black magic, even in a seemingly minor way, is dangerous, but also because of the wrongness of catching and killing any sort of creature for such purposes. One person, however, said that God gave man dominion over the Earth and everything on it, and if people were stupid enough to believe in witchcraft and hand over vast sums of money for an animal that served no "other purpose", he saw no reason not to do it.

That shut me up for a while. I've heard very similar arguments from staunch Christians about the mass production of meat, feathers, cosmetics, and medicine, with the only differences being the witchcraft element. Apparently God is totally okay with the way we toss billions of baby male chicks per year in the egg industry into meat grinders, alive. He's also quite cool with the billions of other animals raised in appalling conditions and then slaughtered in what we call humane ways, but don't appear to be remotely so when actually witnessed. Also added into this justification, is the fact that animals don't have souls. It says so in the bible! Apart from Fido and Kitty of course. Of *course* they have souls—you can see it in their eyes, and they will be waiting for us when we get to heaven. Pardon me while I step away for a really big chuckle.

Go forth and multiply. Kill for fabulous cuisine, great eiderdowns, and wondrous fashion, torture, stuff your faces with absolutely everything—go on—do it!

So it is written. Actually, so it is not written. There are places in the bible that specifically tell us to care for and respect animals. Most of us prefer to focus on the bits of it that tell us that eating animals is exactly what God wants us to do. Which is fair enough. I have yet to see anywhere in any holy book that justifies factory farming, circuses, or the "work" that modern animals are required to do. I'm sure that our God of love is not happy about any of that.

How do we define having a soul? Being sentient? Having feelings, emotions—being capable of love? Some people believe that everything has some degree of life—even rocks and trees. Others believe that only humans have souls. Regardless of what the truth actually is, if we don't live according to what we *know,* no matter how deeply we try to bury that knowing, we will always be at least somewhat out of balance. The problem is that allowing that little *knowing* to emerge all the way enough for us to focus on it would cause us discomfort, and possibly mean us changing our lifestyles in ways that we don't want to change. Worse still, it could mean that we might feel obligated as some point to share what we know, and thereby most definitely either offend, irritate, or enrage others.

For every beast of the forest is mine, the cattle on a thousand hills. I know all the birds of the hills, and all that moves in the field is mine.

Psalm 50 10 - 11

When you look at all the problems around the globe individually, while deeply disturbing, they don't appear to hold the possibility of absolute disaster. If you gather them all together however, taking every aspect of the way we live our lives and the state of the planet into account, there seems to be no possibility of avoiding disaster from this point onwards if we do not change quickly. Whether or not we are already beyond the tipping point or not is not something I know—I hope not, but I'm worried, as are many many others. While reading science-fiction books about heroes having fights with laser guns in domes in between munching on plants grown indoors with not a creature in sight can be exciting, it is not a future life I would want for myself or anyone else. Data is real, and going by the data that is available it is crystal clear that we can't carry on the way we are. It is pointless arguing that climate change is not real, because—well—data. It is pointless arguing that we haven't pretty much destroyed the environment of this planet, because—well—eyeballs. We are a most destructive species. Our consumption of everything is insane, especially our consumption and use of animals.

PEOPLE LOVE ALL CREATURES GREAT AND SMALL

This is the longest chapter in this book because changing our views on the things that follow is going to be the most important step in saving this world and ourselves. Apart from climate change and the other things threatening our continued existence as a species on this planet, as individuals we must begin to live in love, and to live in love we must know what is true. I realise that these things may be difficult to read if you haven't read of them before, but please do try.

The greatness of a nation and its moral progress can be judged by the way in which its animals are treated.

If the thought of reading about such things makes you want to skip this chapter, either because you're afraid it will hurt, or because you think that there is no such thing and everything in the world is just as it should be, then you especially really, *really*, need to read it. Please read it. *Avoidance of any part of the whole of the lives that we live, any part or any aspect, will not allow us to ever truly be whole.* Put your current beliefs on the subject aside while you do so. Try to read from a point of logic and truth rather than emotion. No anger—no guilt—no fear—no heebie jeebies—especially no anger. Just truth. We have all the creatures of this Earth, and all of the Earth itself, in our power at this point in our history, and what we do from this point on is of vital importance, not only to us as the human race, but to each and every one of us as individuals. If you believe that you can make no difference to what happens to billions of animals then you are wrong. Every one good thing that you do for animals—every *single* thing—no matter how insignificant you think it is—is nothing short of a blessing for all of them and all of us. Be strong and read on—this is a long one.

We make a couple of mistakes when it comes to non-human beings. We like to think that it's good for them to live with, or for, us rather than live and die in the wild, and we think that because we can do whatever we want to with them and to them it's alright to do so. The biggest mistake of all is when we convince ourselves that they are not sentient, followed shortly by our beliefs that certain creatures are nobler than others, and so should never be eaten, killed or abused in any way. We are apparently the bestowers of souls as we see fit, and we stubbornly refuse to look further than the point where we have decided which creatures do have them and which don't. At some level we know that if we look deeper than this point we might have to decide differently. Worse—we might have to do something that will remove us from our comfort zone. One amazing truth though, is that nothing worth accomplishing is done in comfort zones.

I have gone way beyond being called a tree-hugger or greenie or worse—it bothers me not at all. I would much rather not be targeted or be thought of as a weirdo, but I always believe what I see, hear, and know—logic is a wonderful thing when we listen to it properly, So fine, call me anything at all for saying out loud what is so very logical if we would take the time to look. The problem with animals at this point in our world's history is the enormous scale at which things are being done to them by us or on our behalf, and the perceived suffering to ourselves that we believe will happen if we suddenly have to go without the things we've come to depend on that we get from them one way or another.

Life, suffering, and death are very much part of our current reality. Every single thing begins to live here and then goes through various joys and pains before they die. You are not likely to ever see anyone on their deathbed after a long and painful illness saying how fabulous it all was and how happy they are to be approaching the point where they will stop breathing and expire. People, animals, fish, insects, reptiles, and every other being all try very hard not to die while enjoying their lives here as much as they can. If you want to boil life here down to two things those are them. To enjoy an abundant and happy life and keep it going for as long as is non-painfully possible.

We don't know anything for sure. We don't know what happens to us when we die, and we don't know what happens to animals when they die. Believing that they don't have souls justifies anything at all that we choose to do to them in our minds. Humans are very good at latching on to beliefs that will make what we *want* to do seem quite alright to do. I emphasise *want* to do because we don't *need* to *do*, or *have done to*, any of the things that we are currently doing to animals. We will be quite alright if we leave them all alone in the wilderness. There are a whole lot of extremely healthy, muscular, and satiated vegans to prove that. I have climbed on and fallen off the vegan wagon for years, so I am not trying to be holier than thou when I mention these things. I never ate meat because I needed the protein—there are very many non-animal sources of protein—I ate meat because I liked eating it. I've eaten a lot of creatures during the course of my life, from prawns to pigs, and every time it was only because they tasted good to me.

Maybe if I'd known that thinking about how they lived and died before I ate them would put me off continuing to do so, I would have tried harder to hang on to the belief that they didn't feel a thing when they got killed after living extremely happy and long lives frolicking in meadows. There are no "food" animals that lead happy or long lives—their existences are just different levels of pain, terror, and entrapment. The only mercy for them is that they don't in fact get to live that way for very long. Young meat is tender and tastier than old meat. These are simple truths—simple facts, and it is not logical to pretend that they are not. Still with me? Breathe, and keep the emotions at bay.

Animals do not want to live with us. That is a fact. Logic once again tells us that rather than trying to get into our homes and insert themselves in solitary splendour in cages or fish tanks or whatever other of the things we use to stop them from running away, they try their level best to get away from us until they are too confused, brainwashed, or terrified to try. Cows do not nobly surrender their lives or their babies so that we can enjoy a nice piece of cheese or fillet steak. They do it because they can't get away. They want what all of us want—to live without being captive and tortured. If you take the time to consider the idiocy of being appalled at the thought of eating dogs while being totally fine with the horrific lives and deaths of "food" animals so that we can eat them you will see that there truly is no difference in the sentience of the species, merely in the way we have been taught to think, and the fact that we don't have cows as pets. If we did we would not want to eat them or wear their skins.

There is a lot of love within many of us for various animals as we go through life, because so many of us bring them into our homes and lives, and make them parts of our families. And when you add human ingredients such as love, selfishness, and the education we get, you will eventually get sadness, grief, and guilt. It's one thing to see animals dying in horrible ways in nature documentaries, but another entirely when these things happen right in front of us to creatures we love intensely.

There are levels of empathy—awareness—levels of consciousness. I've often wondered what goes on in the heads of people who work in abattoirs—those guys who are first in the process of turning live lambs into roasts. So I did a little research. I thought that they must all be just a little bit psychopathic to kill so much every day. I was in for a surprise. While no doubt there are some twisted individuals who have no compassion, and indeed get some sort of kick inflicting pain, and killing, the people who work in these places are not all bloodthirsty maniacs. Some seem to become that way after working there a while though. More and more is being learned about mental illness, and now variations of Post Traumatic Stress Disorder (PTSD) are being found with terrifying regularity. Perpetration Induced Traumatic Stress disorder (PITS) is one of them. While PTSD in most of its forms is brought on by extreme trauma or shock *to* victims, PITS is caused by *causing* extreme trauma—or death. People afflicted with PITS are mainly those whose work sometimes includes causing these things in socially acceptable ways. Members of the police and armed forces come to mind first. The damage done to victims of trafficking who are forced to kill as child soldiers is appalling.

Veterinarians on a much lesser scale have also been found to suffer from PITS. Some of these people kill at least one other being intentionally during the course of their lives because it is part of their job, and this can cause *them* trauma.

Slaughterhouse workers on the other hand kill thousands on a daily basis. The majority of them don't grow up dreaming of working in this capacity. Many of them are financially forced to take whatever work they can get. They're just doing what appears to be the only thing that they can do to care for their families. Slaughterhouse work has been linked to a selection of horrible mental disorders in addition to PITS, and also to alcohol and drug abuse—and violence, among other things. Just as being subjected to constant or repetitive abuse for years will lead to guaranteed damage to victims, constant or repetitive *perpetration* of trauma or killing will lead to the same in previously "normal" people. According to Rachel M Macnair, author of *Perpetration Induced Traumatic Stress: The Psychological Consequences of Killing*, symptoms can include dissociation, depression, panic, and a sense of disintegration.

Many of these workers develop a hatred of themselves and experience a crisis of their own identity—a change in self. They are forced change—to not care. Otherwise they would not be able to do their jobs. The late Virgil Butler who worked in a poultry slaughterhouse for five years before becoming a vocal animal activist said "The sheer amount of killing and blood can really get to you after a while. Especially if you can't just shut down all emotion and turn into a robot zombie of death. Sometimes weird thoughts will enter your head. It's just you and the dying chickens. The surreal feelings grow into such a horror of the barbaric nature of your behaviour. You are murdering helpless birds by the thousands—up to 90,000 a night. You are a killer." In his blog *Cyberactivist*, Butler described other workers pulling heads off live chicken and using them as finger puppets, as well as other unimaginable abuses. He said that apart from the desperate people, who sometimes couldn't even write, taking on this work, that people who already were criminals gravitated towards it. They didn't have problems doing the work. His conscience tormented him though, as theirs did to many others.

Before his sad passing in 2006 he said, "You feel isolated from society—not part of it. Alone. You know you are different from most people. They don't have visions of horrible death in their heads. They have not seen what you have seen. And they don't want to. They don't even want to hear about it."

And there is the rub. We don't want to see it or hear about it, but we find it acceptable that it is being done. If we didn't we wouldn't carry on as we are.

You have just dined, and however scrupulously the slaughterhouse is concealed in the graceful distance of miles, there is complicity.

Ralph Waldo Emerson

Truthfully, it is impossible to be completely vegan on this world at this point. Flocks of thousands of birds are poisoned for eating growing wheat. Not a nice way to die either. Hundreds of thousands of animals die to make way for the planting of some new health food fad that is also vegan. Palm oil, almonds, cashews. Animals die in droves every day for things wanted by people who would never dream of ever eating meat or actual animal products. Harming them the way that we are is not only about eating meat. There is no corner of Earth where we haven't caused trauma or death to some living thing, and we do so every single day.

In our modern world there are many people who have little or nothing to do with animals other than to have them as pets, ornaments, test subjects, to eat them or make use of bits of them in other ways in various products, or simply to have exterminated the ones we don't like. I want to talk about them as being integral to our own wholeness though, because the way they affect us and the way we affect them says a lot about who we are, both as individuals and as a species. I want to talk about them because a lot of what is happening is due to millions of people being unaware of what is actually being done. Knowledge is power, and humans need to begin to find their power as individuals first. Going through life with blinkers on is not the way to do that.

We need to own what we do or *cause* to be done rather than refusing to see it, because as we know, refusing to see something does not make it disappear. It merely lurks in the shadows. The truth is that while birds, hamsters, goldfish, and other creatures might sometimes enrich our lives with their presence, we *never* actually enrich theirs. We steal from them the right to a natural life, to freedom of choice, to do what they were designed to do—to have families, to eat what they want, to fly, run, swim, enjoy, and to live and die as they are entitled to do.

Until one has loved an animal, a part of one's soul remains unawakened

Anatole France

Somewhere along the line we humans have taken on the belief that anything that isn't as clever or "civilised" or not "in possession of a soul" is open season as far as the way we use and treat them. I don't know at what point we got to decide who or what is in possession of sentience, or a soul, or not but I'm pretty sure that we've missed the mark quite disastrously in this respect. One very much ignored point is that animals feel emotions, and it is normal for all sentient beings to feel emotion. If you were not self-aware you would not have feelings of jealousy and love. So, if self-aware means that you have a soul, animals most certainly do have them. If you take the time to look, you will see that they love, they sometimes dislike, they get sad—just like we do. They enjoy and feel joy. They taste. They feel.

We judge the value of the lives of animals and how we treat them in terms of whether they're specifically bred to be food, whether they're pet animals, and also by their quantities, their looks, their actions. How their actions can impact us as well. If birds or rabbits eat our crops they're classified as vermin. If they are our pets they have souls. There are laws that protect most animals from cruelty *other than* those in the food industry. Killing "food" creatures is the whole point of it, so anti-cruelty laws there are purposely vague.

Having said that, I must say that many poor people in third world countries are vegan not by choice but because of severe financial constraints, and vegetables can generally be home-grown in such places. To be a vegan by choice in the Western world and still enjoy all of your meals is not always affordable. Tasty things that can quell those cravings for cheese and meat are not always cheap. The way foods are produced, even if they should have nothing at all to do with animal parts means that many supposedly vegetable based items actually do contain things that are not on the vegan menu. Choices for poor people constrain them to whatever they can afford that will give them the most bang for their buck. They're buying cheap meats stuffed full of antibiotics, chemicals, and the high levels of those hormones released when extreme states of terror and pain are reached during the most cost-effective processing of these animals. They must choose cheap vegetables, pulses, and fruit well past their just picked, vitamin rich fresh prime, once again filled with chemicals and poisons. For such people to go vegan is much more of a challenge than for those who can afford organic, poison-free, meat substitutes and delicious non-animal cheeses.

Still—people do it. Rich people and poor people, once they get to the point of understanding that consuming meat, water creatures, milk, and eggs means that some animals led horrible lives and then were purposely killed find that they just don't want to do it anymore. Do they still crave bacon and pizza? Of course they do. Do they slip now and then? Probably. The point is that once anyone with a degree of reasoning ability and empathy properly looks at these things, they will try to, at the very least, cut down on their animal consumption, use of down feather products, cosmetics and other household items that have been tested on animals, and so on.

When you are poor, or even more difficult, are poor and have a large family to feed and support, it is understandable that taking our very human stance of refusing to look at how these products are obtained is the norm. Why look at something that will give you pain and guilt when there is not much you can do about it? It's easier to follow those tough people who insist that the way we produce our food is quite acceptable, natural, and the way that normal, sane human beings live. It's easier to label those who choose to try and get people to stop the terrible torture inflicted on billions of animals every day as lunatics and weirdos, than to realise that the truth is that any society who would actually condone what is done in the processes of acquiring our foods, fluffy pillows, warm jerseys, and all the rest of the mountains of things that we "need" to survive, is a very weird and lunatic society. Personally I find people who are squeamish with the carving up of a raw chicken or the handling of raw meat, while quite happy to eat quantities of it when it no longer looks so much like dead flesh, beyond irritating. We need to at least have the courage of our convictions, and do boldly what we have *chosen* to do, whatever that is. I have a lot more respect for someone who goes out with a gun and shoots an animal quickly and cleanly, and then uses as much of the carcass as possible, than for anyone who would rather condone the much worse treatment and deaths of captive animals bred to eat while refusing to examine what is done in the process. If you couldn't bring yourself to kill it, why on Earth are you prepared to eat it after someone else has?

Before you rush off and call me a vegan nutjob in a blistering review on Amazon, please note that I have almost always been one of the weirdo lunatics who have turned a blind eye to what happens to the animals I have eaten or delighted in the beauty of their skins when turned into a fabulous handbag. I have dissected thousands of chickens and personally butchered hindquarters of various animals, from sheep to cows. The realisations that these things are wrong— and that they are also *choices* that I haven't had to make—have come to me slowly over the years. Insistent little *knowings* that I haven't always been able to ignore. So while now I try not to be part of these systems of the pain, terror, and death of creatures just because I can and because I want gorgeous or tasty things, I don't always get it right. How we live is personal—we decide what we believe, one way or another, and truthfully in the end we pretty much only have to answer to ourselves. I'm not writing these things to make anyone feel condemned. The societies and systems we were all born into have all been well entrenched for a very long time, and it will take individual, personal reflection, and the one by one decisions made over time before such powerful established ways of doing things will be changed.

Even though it may take decades, I think that most of us don't want anything to be so badly treated for our own use. Sooner or later humanity, or whatever is left of it at the rate we're going now, will be kinder, stronger, and able to make decisions that do not actually deprive us of pleasure for the benefit of other living souls, who truthfully do not owe us anything—not their bodies, their feathers, their bodily fluids or eggs, and most certainly not their right to lives lived joyfully and naturally on this world that we seem to believe belongs to us alone, when it really does not. For now, every one time we choose not to partake in anything animal is a victory, and does not have to entail the immediate and vociferous change to being vegan. Every one of these singular times that we choose one vegan day a week is going to be a triumph. Remember that even though there is only one of you, there are a whole lot of other ones doing the same thing, so the statement "well, the animal is dead already" only means that with less people buying these "already dead" animals will ensure that less of them need to be bred and slaughtered in the future. Baby steps are good enough, and most certainly better than no steps at all.

If the goal of our human soul is to learn to love unconditionally, how is it then that we think that animal souls are less important than ours—or even non-existent, when they are born masters of unconditional love?

We humans can justify most things that we *want* to do, and that's what most of the things that we do come down to—we do them because we *want* to do them. We might convince ourselves that we have no choice in our actions, but we almost always do. Even atheists latch on to passages from the bible to show that it is our God-given right to eat animals. At the end of everything, nothing matters except what you feel in your heart. If something feels wrong to you then it is wrong for you. It doesn't matter how loud and sensible the arguments are for doing whatever, and even if giving up something is hard for you, sometimes that is the path to take for the health of your own soul.

All of life is precious, and everything deserves to live its life out according to its own desires, with at least a fighting chance at happiness and freedom while it does so. There is no verse in the bible, or any other holy book for that matter, that condones what we collectively are doing to this planet and the sentient creatures on it today. There are indeed verses that state that we should be kind to the animals in our care. In actuality we have created a living hell for billions of creatures from their birth to their death—and it is not right or acceptable in any way.

PEOPLE CAN BEGIN AGAIN

Imperfection is Perfect. That's it. What most of us are waiting for is perfection. We can't move forward until this happens or that is in place. We can't start a business because we have no capital, or education, or premises, or whatever. The dusting must be done before we can vacuum. We must wait for confirmation that we have our new job before we can have fun. When there's something horrible looming also, we feel that we must put living on hold until it passes. We postpone our happiness with beliefs such as "I can't be happy till I find love" "I can't be happy until I lose fifty pounds" "I can't be happy till my daughter stops taking drugs". You can actually. You can be happy any time you like. There's no need to wait for anything. When we learn that life isn't meant to be perfect, and that it's alright to move on from all sorts of perceived imperfection, that's when the fun begins. When we realise that it is entirely possible to spend our whole lives waiting for something or other to happen and never enjoying the moment—never enjoying what we have now. There's always something good in now, no matter how small, and if we choose to focus on that rather than what might or might not happen at some future point we are throwing away the time of our life.

Work is seldom always easy and fun, even when it is doing the work of your calling or dream. You will notice that some of the most outrageous rags to riches success don't come from people who had loads of cash to begin with. Often these people didn't have much of a traditional education, and the dreams that they started out with weren't necessarily to make a pile of cash. They had goals—things that they wanted to accomplish because of a burning desire—they wanted to live the life that they felt called to live. The cash was a by-product of them having the discipline to act every day towards achieving their goals. Personal goals. They bucked the system and carved their own roads. And so must all of us begin to take responsibility for ourselves at the very least.

Remember, the part of us that we imagine needs healing is not the part we create from; that part is far deeper and stronger. The part we create from can't be touched by anything our parents did, or society did. That part is unsullied, uncorrupted; soundproof, waterproof, and bulletproof. In fact, the more troubles we've got, the better and richer that part becomes.

Pressfield, Steven. The War of Art (pp. 48-49). Black Irish Entertainment LLC. Kindle Edition.

If nothing in life was hard then everyone would be writing symphonies, writing bestsellers, and always doing the right things. Great symphonies are not easy to write. They can take years of slogging away—putting in hours that you don't want to put in—going without the things you could be enjoying if you took a more mainstream approach to living your life. Creating beauty and doing worthwhile things is always hard work precisely because doing them is not what is easiest. Humans, with our inner fears and criticisms, can sometimes find it hard to simply get up in the mornings. When we are faced with the choice of facing things that terrify us and doing the hard things it takes a lot out of us, and mostly we look for some less scary path to follow. The few who don't are the ones who write symphonies even though they are blind. They write the books that change lives. They find cures for what ails us and create artistic majesty in many forms.

Sometimes the hard things never leave anything physical after we're gone. Sometimes the hard things are as simple as finding our true selves and living joyfully. But every one of the hard things done is worthwhile for the whole world, because even joy is shared in the very air we all breathe. In the end, no matter how much of a grip evil has gained on this world, it can be overcome completely by one human. You. Every single human on this planet has the free will to reject it in their own lives, and each rejection will form the landslide that can wash clean the Earth of it.

And so we have delved into some of our secrets. The secrets of humans. Those things that we hide away, from ourselves or others or both. People have many more secrets, and the object of writing this book was to hopefully encourage some to step out on a path of discovery. To realise that maybe this life should not only be about houses and cars and clothes. To understand that maybe the really valuable things for us to acquire while we are here are not physically tangible. To see that love is not only to be given to our direct family and friends, but to all. To respect the world that we are on and the creatures who share it with us. To see that there are always choices. That good is real, and that evil is real, and that we choose every second of our lives whether or not to add victories to one or the other. In beginning with small personal choices chances are that humanity will soon be able to join together and make choices for the good of all. For good. For love.

RECOMMENDED READING

The Secret of the Shadow Debbie Ford

The Shadow Effect Deepak Chopra Debbie Ford Marianne Williamson

Healing Trauma through Self-Parenting Patricia O'Gorman, Ph D and Phil Diaz M.S.W

Becoming Supernatural Dr Joe Dispenza

Why We Love Dogs Eat Pigs and Wear Cows Melanie Joy Ph D

The People of the Lie Dr M Scott Peck

The War of Art Steven Pressfield

The Gifts of Imperfection Brené Brown Ph D, L.M.S.W

Waking the Tiger Peter Levine

The Body Keeps the Score Dr Bessel van der Kolk

Perpetration Induced Traumatic Stress: The Psychological Consequences of Killing Rachel M Macnair

OTHER BOOKS BY JO ROBINSON

African Me & Satellite TV

Echoes of Narcissus in the Gardens of Delight

Sands of Time

Fly Birdie

The Visitation

Nkoninkoni

9780639948881